THEME
Play

THEME
Play .... ●

Exciting Young Imaginations

GARY ZINGHER

Foreword by
Augustus Trowbridge

LIBRARIES
UNLIMITED
A Member of the Greenwood Publishing Group
Westport, Connecticut • London

Library of Congress Cataloging-in-Publication Data

Zingher, Gary.
  Theme play : exciting young imaginations / by Gary Zingher ; foreword by
Augustus Trowbridge.
    p. cm.
  Includes bibliographical references and index.
  ISBN 1–59158–307–1 (pbk. : alk. paper)
  1. Play. 2. Early childhood education—Activity programs. 3. Drama in
education. 4. Imagination in children. 5. Effective teaching. I. Title.
LB1139.35.P55Z56 2006
649'.51–dc22   2006012718

British Library Cataloguing in Publication Data is available.

Library of Congress Catalog Card Number: 2006012718
ISBN: 1–59158–307–1

First published in 2006

Libraries Unlimited, 88 Post Road West, Westport, CT 06881
A Member of the Greenwood Publishing Group, Inc.
www.lu.com

Printed in the United States of America

The paper used in this book complies with the
Permanent Paper Standard issued by the National
Information Standards Organization (Z39.48–1984).

10 9 8 7 6 5 4 3 2 1

To
  Miguel, Ariana, Josh, Katie, and Julio

CONTENTS ···●

ACKNOWLEDGMENTS ·····································•

Much of what is presented in this book is distilled from my column, "Thematic Journeys," written over the last ten years for *School Library Media Activities Monthly*. The children of Corlears School and Manhattan Country School in New York City inspired many of these themes and projects, and included in this work are samples of their writing.

I would especially like to thank Paula Montgomery, who encouraged the creation of this book; Dulce Moche, who helped me in shaping the material; Ernest Burgos for all his technical wizardry; Bonnie Levine for collaborating with me on so many magical journeys; my mother, Fran Zingher, who nourished my own imagination; and the teachers of both Corlears and Manhattan Country School for being so open and adventurous.

I would also like to acknowledge the following individuals for their enthusiasm and support: Moses Gardner, Donna Novak, Adam Bender, Gail Martell, John Block, Gus and Marty Trowbridge, Cynthia Rogers, Kallyn Krash, Jean Finnerty, Linda Winston, Thya Merz, Romy Romero, Karen Segal, Sandy Lewin, Louise Matteoni, Lois Greenfield, Rose Pappalardo, Pam Rausch, Karen Ruelle, and Irv Topal.

And, finally, I wish to express my appreciation to Max, Paul, and Malcom Kuemmerlein, who often encounter squires and dragons.

FOREWORD ●

Theme Play: Exciting Young Imaginations is as compelling as the journeys Gary Zingher leads with children, an itinerary, like a treasure map, for those who never had him as a teacher. His thesis, entitled "The Relevance of Thematic Journeys," tucked into two pithy paragraphs at the end of Chapter 2, warrants universal reflection.

It is children's innate sense of possibility that Gary taps, and he enlists them in collaborative experiences that build bridges to other worlds and viewpoints, a gift that will nourish them and radiate for a lifetime.

At a time when competition trumps cooperation and monocultures discourage individuality, many children will find themselves left behind. Gary shows us how to balance the scales for the benefit of all.

A person of extraordinary talent, Gary's contributions to education deserve to be shared with educators far beyond those associated with one school. He was librarian for Manhattan Country School from 1983 to 1994, when he chose to leave his work to pursue his writing and research.

While a trained librarian with an extensive knowledge of children's literature, Gary is foremost a teacher, uniquely gifted in developing the imaginations and creativity of children. His book documents his work so well that it would not do him justice for me to describe his methodology.

I can say, however, unlike any teacher I have known, Gary inspires and leads children to explore their ideas and emotions, to love language, and to think and to express themselves with originality and feeling. The response of children to Gary's teaching is so creative and productive that it is as if they are under a spell, yet Gary is never controlling. More likely, his technique is the opposite.

Gary adores stories, fanciful plots, and thematic complexities, and when he teaches, he becomes intellectually intimate with children, encouraging them to open and extend their minds and to delight in their own "journeys." He also engages children to work collaboratively, to inspire each other, and to produce jointly developed projects. In this fashion, Gary is more the orchestrator than the conductor, and the children themselves are free to experiment and feed on each other's imaginations.

Gary's program always extends beyond the library directly into the classrooms. He works closely with teachers, inventively designing projects that enrich the classroom curriculum with culminating activities such as plays and other dramatic presentations. In fact, the library becomes the creative center of the school and is a powerful resource in voicing the expression of children throughout the school.

As an educator with such a depth of understanding of child development, Gary has been an invaluable colleague to teachers seeking to know children better and to meet their needs with greater sensitivity and effectiveness. Like Will Rogers, one could say that Gary perhaps never met a child he did not like. And so is the reverse. Children adore him and seize every opportunity to be with him in ways that seem more play than work.

Theme Play: Exciting Young Imaginations will energize practitioners to create new programs by tapping into the book's powerful themes. Gary Zingher offers a playful approach to helping children define who they are and investigate the worlds they inhabit. Furthermore, the book conveys the author's humor and spirit, as well as his sense of possibility and adventure. At its core, it is really a book about developing creative thinkers with compassionate hearts and launching them on lifelong explorations.

Augustus Trowbridge
Founder and Director Emeritus of Manhattan Country School

PREFACE ··· ●

As an offbeat kid growing up in Kansas City, I was described as a "dreamer," someone whose head was tickling the clouds. I remember spending hours in both my bedroom and my backyard hideout writing poems and stories and sometimes thinking up scenarios for films, even dramatizing them with handpicked flower puppets.

Saturdays were heaven for a kid like me. In the morning, on my white Sears radio, I would listen to the story anthology *Let's Pretend*. In the afternoon, I would attend the matinee at the Southtown, only seven blocks away.

For thirty-five cents, I could delight in the images of Robin Hood, Long John Silver, Annie Oakley, and the metallic giant Gort from *The Day the Earth Stood Still*. Many times I had nightmares featuring this eight-foot-tall robot, and I quickly learned those critical words—"Gort! Klaatu barada nikto," spoken by the Patricia Neal character—that I knew would always protect me.

All the pretending and writing I did were tied to my own private sphere and were never once connected to school. In the classroom I felt awkward and edgy, as if I was locked in my seat and had to put everything on hold. For me, school was about having illegible handwriting, the messiest desk in my row, and being picked second to last in kickball games.

Still, there were some bright spots—a fourth-grade substitute who would tell stories about Sherlock Holmes and Moriarity and this marvelous troupe of women who would come each year to dramatize one of Grimm's fairy tales. These plays were humorous and enthralling and introduced me to the magical vehicle of live theater.

Not until I was 11 years old, attending summer camp, did I feel safe enough to express my poetic self in the outside world. In this informal setting, where you could be high-spirited and zany and not get into trouble, I found peers to collaborate with when creating skits for various camp programs. I was the catalyst, the "concept" guy, and others looked to me for inspiration and direction.

I also wrote articles and stories for the camp newspaper, and this experience empowered me immensely. All of a sudden, I was less shy and more confident and had friends and appreciators; a unique little butterfly had begun to emerge.

It is not ironic that nine summers later I would be working as a counselor for inner-city children at a sleepaway camp in New Jersey. This turned out to be a defining summer as well–a summer where important things crystallized and I realized my calling.

Here, in our unit lodge, I developed my first Imagination Center as an alternative to the recreational swim. At the center, campers could explore such powerful themes as Humor, Survival, and Science Fiction through discussion, dramatic play, story writing, bookmaking, movement, and various art activities. At the end of each session, we would come together, and the children would share their creations.

At first only seven campers came, and these were kids with head colds and poison ivy. But by the next week, word had spread, and as many as twenty-one kids signed up and were willing to forgo their afternoon dip in the lake. A second counselor was now assigned to work with me.

Each session, I sensed the children's excitement in having this chance to extend their imaginations and communicate their poetry and feelings. In this makeshift center, they were listened to and encouraged. It was definitely a learning place, but unlike school.

Somehow I was able to create an atmosphere in which children were motivated to explore and express thoughts that were basic to their own lives. Intuitively, I knew how to set the tone, ignite the spark, and introduce them to whole new realms. As a facilitator, I could help them to share and work with each other in ways that were generous and respectful.

That summer my professional odyssey truly began. Even though arts-in-education programs and degrees did not yet exist, I was committed to developing Imagination Centers wherever I could. I wanted to create worlds where children could experiment and make believe–worlds that were thoughtful and playful and where I, as a child, would have flourished.

Throughout the last forty years, I have been able to implement my vision in a number of settings. In the roles of camp arts director, play therapist, after-school leader, imagination consultant, and library media specialist, I have been able to expand children's experiences by combining human concerns, literature, and the creative arts.

As a catalyst, I have been able to tap into the imagination of children, sparking ideas for projects that hit the center of children's interests as well as their sense of fun and adventure. I respect what children know and wonder about and try to stir up their natural curiosities, encouraging them to ask a million questions and then helping them to find the connections and answers within themselves.

In the Imagination Workshops I have led and college courses I have instructed, I have seen practitioners start to play with these themes, recognizing their relevance and power. I have seen their enthusiasm as they thought about adapting them to their own situations and embarking on particular journeys.

All of these themes are universal and evolving–lifelong themes that one can return to without ever depleting the well of possibilities. These are my riches, the themes I have collected and nurtured. It now seems the time to send them out into the world, hoping that others will embrace them.

Embarking with Children
on Thematic Journeys

What are the powerful themes of childhood, and why do they touch children so deeply? How might these themes transport children and allow them to journey with their imaginations? In what ways can professionals who work with children use these themes to develop thoughtful and creative programs and units of study? These are the major questions this book addresses.

To begin with, one needs to be attuned to children in all their contexts, entering their worlds, observing their games, and listening to their conversations. Through this kind of engagement, one might get to know the stories they like to tell, the experiences they value, the things they worry about, the ways they spend their free time, and the treasures they carry in their pockets.

Themes that resonate with children are the ones that touch the heart of childhood and stimulate both inquiry and poetic expression. Any of the themes introduced in this book can invigorate a program, and each theme explored will yield its own pleasures and truths. Practitioners can introduce these themes in a variety of settings—elementary school classrooms, resource rooms, school and public libraries, camps, after-school centers, and pediatric playrooms.

Tricks and Tricksters

The theme of Tricks and Tricksters, for example, appeals to all age-groups. Children love putting on magic shows. They take pleasure in learning new tricks and then trying them out on their friends. They are curious about magicians and the objects they carry in their bags.

Many children might have questions related to the theme that they wish to pursue. What are the tricks of genies, wizards, actors, and jesters? What is a hoax, and what is an illusion? Why do practical jokes sometimes backfire? Who are the tricksters in folktales and fairy tales? How do they use trickery as a survival technique? How might their trickery involve deceiving or flattering others, wearing a disguise, or causing a diversion?

Younger children might want to discuss how and why Miss Nelson became Viola Swamp (Allard) or why the father and son in *Abiyoyo* (Seeger) were ostracized from their town. They might choose to share some of their favorite Halloween tricks and April Fools' Day jokes or put on puppet shows based on Aesop's fables.

Middle-grade children could try out different coin and card tricks or develop a "disappearing act." They could also practice writing with invisible ink, experiment with trick photography, or create a secret code. Some children might want to act out trickster tales from around the world such as *Rabbit Makes a Monkey of Lion* (Aardema) from Africa or *Pedro and the Padre* (Aardema) from Mexico.

Older children could publish a newsletter for young magicians that might include an advice column from Merlin; a copy of Harry Potter's first report card; book reviews of *Half Magic* (Eager), *The Houdini Box* (Selznick), and *The Witches* (Dahl); and an interview with a veteran rabbit who explains the pitfalls of the famous rabbit-in-the-hat trick. They would need to think of a name for their newsletter, perhaps something like *The Magic Eye* or *The Now-You-See-It News*.

Whatever the age-group or setting, this is a capturing theme with a myriad of possibilities. It offers an element of suspense and allows for all kinds of learning. In fact, simply performing a trick requires concentration, timing, and careful execution.

The After-School Reading Club

In my experience over the past forty years, working with children of all ages in many different contexts, I have learned that my own enthusiasm is indispensable in setting the tone and sustaining the children's involvement.

A number of years ago, I advised an after-school reading club at a private school in New York City. The ten enrolled fourth-graders, meeting in the library, came to the first session having read the assigned book, *Tales of a Fourth Grade Nothing* by Judy Blume.

What emerged from our book discussion that first day was how many of these children empathized with the character of Peter, who was constantly annoyed by the antics of his younger brother, Fudge. They especially enjoyed the restaurant scene in which Fudge, an expert mess-maker, treats his food as Play-Doh and invents the "mashed potato smear," using the restaurant wall as his canvas.

Some children then began expressing their own irritations about having a younger sibling, trying to top each other as they exchanged personal anecdotes. ("My little brother is always burping to get attention." "My baby sister likes to wander into my room and hide my things.")

Obviously, this was a chance for them to vent, to release some of their frustrations in the company of peers who listened and completely understood. They all seemed to delight in the telling of their tales, sometimes grimacing, shaking their heads, and rolling their eyes to emphasize their string of displeasures.

Since it was clear to me that talking about annoyances struck a chord with them, I decided to pursue this theme in the following session. The next week, when I suggested that they compile a list of annoying things, they responded immediately.

Someone described the ordeal of waiting in the lice line at school to have her head checked. Another child shared how he hated the shrill, intrusive sound of his alarm clock (but perhaps what he really hated was having to get up early and go to school). All types of things "ticked them off" and "pushed their buttons," so their list grew rather quickly. As one child would add to the list, others would often chime in, "I know just what you mean!"

A List of Annoying Things

Mosquitoes	Ink stains
The sound of a vacuum cleaner	A baby shrieking
Getting told on	Getting one's hair tangled
Having an itch	Having to wear braces
Splinters	Bees at a picnic
Younger siblings	Older siblings
Going to "time out"	Going to the dentist
Loud barking dogs	Losing the remote control
Water dripping at night	Gutter balls in bowling
People who always interrupt	People who joke too much
Not getting called on when you finally know the answer	

In our third session, I suggested that children create a Hall of Fame of annoying characters from books and films. They took turns nominating a character and then persuading others why that character should be selected.

Among those considered were Lucy of the Peanuts gang, Harriet the whiner from *Tales for the Perfect Child* (Heide), the blabbering donkey from *Shrek*, and the outrageous Newman from the *Seinfeld* show. Next they made posters of these characters that were displayed in the library media center.

In our fourth and final session, I divided the children into three groups so they could create mini-dramas about irksome people with irritating habits and personalities. I sensed, at this point, that they were ready to improvise and play off each other.

To set up this activity, children considered a number of character types. These included the attention-getter, the busybody, the pessimist, the name-dropper, and the know-it-all.

Once in their groups, they thought about what role they wanted to assume. For the settings of their skits, they chose (from a suggested list) a stagecoach, an elevator that was stuck, and the ticket line outside a movie theater.

Finally, when the plays were presented, children conveyed the comical aspects of what might happen when annoying people are forced to interact. One could see their confidence and delight and how immersed they were in playing their roles. They loved performing and were generous as audience members.

This thematic exploration seemed to engage children fully. The sharing of certain frustrations proved to be cathartic for them, and they were often reassured by the support of the group. Furthermore, all of these activities enabled children to express their humor, to collaborate, and to be inventive.

Our discussions provoked some serious thought about why individuals reacted differently to particular annoyances. Not all children were irritated when a parent snored. Not all children minded if they had to clear the table.

We also examined how being annoyed might be tied to other emotions. Wearing braces, for example, could make one feel awkward or self-conscious. Having hiccups at school could be embarrassing. Getting gutter balls in bowling could diminish one's self-esteem.

Tales of a Fourth Grade Nothing had been a splendid starting point for a literacy-based, open-ended journey. Right away, it pulled the children in and piqued their curiosity. It was easy for them to empathize with its hero, Peter, and all the ways he reacted to the annoying Fudge, and it was easy for me to see, in reviewing that first discussion, the potential of this powerful theme.

All the activities that followed came from the children's interest in and response to the literature. They were not preplanned but evolved spontaneously. In explorations such as these, practitioners will need to "go with the flow" and let their own creativity emerge.

How Journeys Begin

The starting point of any journey is where the child and the theme first connect. It is the hook, the heart-stone, the bridge to further exploration. Whatever way a journey begins, it should draw children in at once, inviting them to raise questions, probe further, and make their own discoveries. It must engage, entice, and set the mood, sparking their sense of adventure.

Almost anything can be a starting point. A journey might begin with one child sharing a dream, memory, or an entire group learning a folkdance. It can begin with a pantomime, a fortune cookie, a video, a drawing of a gargoyle, a science experiment, or a special guest or visitor.

Possible Starting Points

Something read aloud or told	*A sensory experience*
A picture book	Analyzing a painting
A family story	Going on a blind walk
A poem or limerick	Peeking into a peep world
A proverb	Listening to a jazz recording
A joke	Smelling a mysterious spice
A prediction	Tasting a French pastry
A diary entry	Identifying night sounds
A paper treasure	*An object or prop*
A map	A kaleidoscope
A menu	A key

A postcard	A honeycomb
A theater program	A sand dollar
A photograph	A button
A swimming certificate	A compass
A family recipe	A locket

A puzzler	*A creative activity*
A riddle	Writing a parody
A maze	Making up a chant
A code	Mixing a brew
A magic trick	Doing an improvisation
A brainteaser	Inventing a toy
A word game	Designing a hideout
A droodle	Creating a radio play

What happens in the beginning matters immensely. This is the launching period, and something must ignite. Often questions raised in the first discussion will be the threads that link all the parts of the journey, determining its direction and the ways it moves and evolves. The five themes introduced below illustrate how varied the starting points can be. The fifth theme, Garden Tours and Adventures, will be elaborated on more fully, showing follow-up activities with children of various ages.

Reveilles and Roundups

The blowing of a ram's horn or shofar could arouse children's curiosity about the kinds of instruments that call people together—instruments such as the bell, bugle, conch, and African drum. When might they be used, and who are the callers? When people hear these sounds, are there certain places where they gather? The books *The Bell Ringer and the Pirates* (Coerr) and *Lord of the Flies* (Golding) each elaborate on this theme, appealing to two very different age-groups.

Baseball and Baseball Lore

A sound recording of Abbott and Costello's "Who's on First?" could excite children to explore the theme of Baseball and Baseball Lore. Books such as *Playing Right Field* (Welch) and *The Field Beyond the Outfield* (Teague) could be used to emphasize the humor in the sport, while *Baseball Saved Us* (Mochizuki) and *Teammates* (Golenbock) treat the subject more seriously. Some children might want to introduce examples of the infield patter they use when playing the game, chants like "We want a pitcher, not a belly itcher!"

Road Trips

The teaching of diner lingo from *Steven Caney's Kids' America* ("stretch" means coke, "a hot dog on wheels" means a hot dog to go) could be the perfect activity to start a thematic journey about family road trips and visits to such offbeat places as an ice-cream museum or alligator farm. Who, in their travels, might have seen an actual two-headed turtle or the world's biggest ball of string? Children could teach each other travel games and share stories about any interesting side trips, detours, or stopovers. Books used to enhance this theme might include *Just Us Women* (Caines), *The Gold Cadillac* (Taylor), and *Stringbean's Trip to the Shining Sea* (Williams, V.).

Toys and Toy Making

The demonstration of a push toy, as illustrated in the picture book *Galimoto* (Williams, K. W.) could introduce children to the theme of Toys and Toy Making. It could encourage them to invent wild and fanciful toys, or perhaps toys of the future. They could then design their own toy catalog. Some children might want to investigate toys lost in time and later unearthed by archeologists in all parts of the world. Among books that explore the toy-making theme are *The Chalk Doll* (Pomerantz), *Daniel's Duck* (Bulla), *Josephine's Imagination* (Dobrin), *Goldie the Dollmaker* (Goffstein), and *Paddle-to-the-Sea* (Holling).

Garden Tours and Adventures

The playing of the Beatles song "The Octopus's Garden" could stimulate children's interest in the theme of Gardens. When they listen to the music, what are the images they see? Is it a whimsical garden with weird-looking fish or perhaps a garden abundant with sea blossoms and sparkling coral? They could bring this garden to life through individual paintings or a collaborative mural.

In sessions that follow, they could examine a number of questions. How does one nurture and maintain a garden? How can this help someone to be caring and productive and more attuned to the earth and the cycles of nature? What insects and animals are garden regulars? What are the famous gardens of the world? Why are gardens often the settings in children's stories?

They could discover different types of gardens as they journey through books, visiting Mr. McGregor's garden in *The Tale of Peter Rabbit* (Potter), the desert garden in *Coyote Dreams* (Nunes), *The Secret Garden* (Burnett), *Tom's Midnight Garden* (Pearce), *The Garden of Abdul Gasazi* (Van Allsburg), and *Linnea in Monet's Garden* (Bjork).

This is a theme that bursts with possibilities for creative expression. Children might want to make button gardens or crystal gardens. They could create a paper-sculpture garden and then celebrate by having high tea or a garden party. Some might be inspired to write haikus after entering the Japanese garden, a place with a wonderful stillness, so exquisitely depicted in the book *In a Spring Garden* (Lewis).

Younger children could become leprechauns and create a special garden where they tend their bed of four-leaf clovers. Visitors might observe them planting, watering, weeding, or perhaps eating green cheese and practicing magic spells with emerald wands.

Middle-grade children could develop little mysteries about garden intruders, "Who goes in my garden? Who steals my corn?" These plays might center on a stranger, a ghost, a scarecrow, or a fox. Someone might even sneak into the garden at night to plant a giant artichoke or an enchanted crop.

Older children might want to design a garden of hats or a garden of sounds or write short stories about a garden of riddles or a garden of dreams. Some children might prefer to read and dramatize James Thurber's witty and ironic short story "The Unicorn in the Garden."

Collaborators on a Journey

The themes presented here transcend times and cultures, linking children to the larger community. They invite children to travel the open road, to be adventurers, to stop from time to time to collect a story or two.

When children embrace a theme and invest in the journey, they may become more passionate readers. Some may want to pursue fictional works that deal with the subject, while others may read information books that focus on the aspects that intrigue them. Books often provide the starting point for many thematic explorations.

This approach invites children to consider all the dimensions of a theme—to raise questions, investigate, play with ideas, develop improvisations and scenarios, and communicate their discoveries in ways that are creative and compelling. It allows them to be both story makers and writers.

For those working with children, this approach involves identifying the theme, choosing the starting point, shaping the journey, and, ideally, celebrating the journey through some type of special program or literacy event. Because thematic journeys are open-ended, practitioners may, at times, need to shift gears, rethink their strategies, and redirect their efforts. But the investment and initial uncertainties are well worth it, for the results can be astonishing.

Each journey involves having a main path in mind, yet a willingness to try out any byways or detours. There is no formula, and some sessions will be richer than others. For every bump or mishap, there are likely to be unanticipated joys. Eventually, practitioners will find their own comfort level and a way of working with themes that is natural for them.

All of these explorations lend themselves to individual adaptation. Although settings differ, there are many common challenges in trying to implement a theme-based program. Practitioners must first consider the logistics—setting up the schedule, arranging the space, and selecting and gathering the materials. They may want to pull in others to assist them: parents, seniors, community people, counselors-in-training, older children, interns, or student teachers.

It seems that the use of themes can be more powerful if they are structured through collaboration with the children and other adults. The adult partnership acts as a model for the children, which helps them learn to collaborate with each other.

What is essential is that the same group of children meets regularly over a period of time so that they will get to know one another as collaborators on a journey. Hopefully, through these experiences, children will learn to be more generous and tolerant and to see everyone as a resource with a unique combination of talents and strengths.

Resources

Books

Aardema, Verna. *Pedro and the Padre*. Dial, 1991.
Aardema, Verna. *Rabbit Makes a Monkey of Lion*. Dial, 1989.
Allard, Harry. *Miss Nelson Is Missing*. Houghton, 1977.
Bjork, Christina. *Linnea in Monet's Garden*. Raben, 1985.
Blume, Judy. *Tales of a Fourth Grade Nothing*. Dutton, 1972.
Bulla, Clyde. *Daniel's Duck*. Harper, 1979.
Burnett, Frances. *The Secret Garden*. Lippincott, 1962.
Caines, Jeannette. *Just Us Women*. HarperCollins, 1984.
Caney, Steven. *Steven Caney's Kids' America*. Workman, 1978.
Coerr, Eleanor. *The Bell Ringer and the Pirates*. HarperCollins, 1983.
Dahl, Roald. *The Witches*. Farrar, 1983.
Dobrin, Arnold. *Josephine's Imagination*. Four Winds, 1973.
Eager, Edward. *Half Magic*. Harcourt, 1964.
Goffstein, M. B. *Goldie the Dollmaker*. Farrar, 1969.
Golding, William. *Lord of the Flies*. Sagebrush, 1999.
Golenbock, Peter. *Teammates*. Gulliver, 1990.
Heide, Florence. *Tales for the Perfect Child*. Morrow, 1985.
Holling, Holling. *Paddle-to-the-Sea*. Houghton, 1988.
Lewis, Richard. *In a Spring Garden*. Dial, 1965.
Mochizuki, Ken. *Baseball Saved Us*. Lee, 1995.
Nunes, Susan. *Coyote Dreams*. Atheneum, 1988.
Pearce, Phillipa. *Tom's Midnight Garden*. Lippincott, 1958.
Pomerantz, Charlotte. *The Chalk Doll*. Lippincott, 1989.
Potter, Beatrix. *The Tale of Peter Rabbit*. Warne, 1903.
Seeger, Pete. *Abiyoyo*. Macmillan, 1986.
Selznick, Brian. *The Houdini Box*. Knopf, 1991.
Taylor, Mildred. *The Gold Cadillac*. Dial, 1987.
Teague, Mark. *The Field Beyond the Outfield*. Scholastic, 1994.
Thurber, James. "The Unicorn in the Garden," in *Fables of Our Time*. Harper, 1983.
Van Allsburg, Chris. *The Garden of Abdul Gazasi*. Houghton, 1979.
Welch, Willie. *Playing Right Field*. Scholastic, 1995.
Williams, Karen W. *Galimoto*. Lothrop, 1990.
Williams, Vera. *Stringbean's Trip to the Shining Sea*. Morrow, 1988.

2

Experimenting with Themes in Different Settings

Preparing the Emotional Setting

In any setting, children need to feel safe and comfortable and will participate more fully if certain needs are met. If they are hungry or tired, their attention may be affected. They may need time to unwind, touch base with a friend, or share a concern with the group leader. Some may be transitioning from a difficult part of the day or struggling with issues brought from home. Attending to these needs, feelings, or preoccupations before the theme is presented is helpful.

Practitioners will need to reassure children that in this setting, it is okay to relax and let go of troubling things. They may want to encourage children in these first few minutes to exchange a few jokes or engage in a short, quiet game.

Preparing the Physical Environment

The development of the physical setting is equally important in helping children relax and focus. There might be special mats to sit on, even large pillows to lie on.

An optimum environment is one that is stimulating, but uncluttered. Materials relating to the theme might be on display to pique the children's interest. Ideally, there are books to read and treasures to examine. Some of these may include discoveries made in previous sessions. All of this helps prepare the group for setting off on a new adventure.

If children, for example, are involved in a thematic journey on Fortune Telling, they could, during this time, examine some theme-related objects in a browsing area. These might include tarot cards, a Ouija board, a Magic 8 Ball, or a book about Greek myths and oracles.

Pulling the Elements Together

Before the children arrive, practitioners must pull these elements together by drawing on their knowledge of group dynamics and children's developmental needs. They must establish rituals, set the tone, and put everyone at ease.

However, not all practitioners will have the time or freedom to prepare the environment and make it their own. This is especially true if they are working in a space they inherited. Group leaders in after-school programs often have only five or ten minutes to set up and prepare a space before the children arrive.

In these situations, group leaders may want to start a session with a quick yoga exercise, a drawing time, or the sharing of a poem. All of these activities help children to settle down and feel connected. Most important, they ensure that the group is emotionally ready to begin or continue their journey.

Launching the Journey

This section of the book examines how particular themes may evolve in different settings. For example, in the course of my work, the theme of Secret Clearings sparked two remarkable journeys, one in a camp and the other in a school library media center.

THEME 1:
Secret Clearings ....●

In a Camp Setting

Years ago, I worked as a camp counselor for a sleepaway camp in New Jersey. One summer, I developed and led a program called the "Into the Woods" hiking club. It was a morning elective that met six times. Our meeting place was a wooden picnic table set in a pine forest.

In our first session, this group of eight 10-year-olds chose to blaze trails and go searching for secret clearings. Most of them, the summer before, had made the trip to Kropsy's clearing–Kropsy being the local scary legend. So now they were hoping to find other clearings–clearings with arrowheads, artifacts, and signs of past human activity. These campers genuinely loved science and nature and began each hike with the spirit of true investigators.

On their first journey, they found in one clearing the tilted foundation of an old brick house, surrounded by yellow wildflowers. In our second meeting, they enjoyed following a creek, but it did not lead to a secret clearing. After some discussion, they decided that the next time they would head toward the rock quarry.

In our third session, they came upon another clearing where they encountered two weathered scarecrows. To the children, these tattered figures were imbued with protective powers and seemed to be the guardians of the clearing.

In the remaining sessions, the hiking club visited each of these two clearings a second time, in order to make sketches of what they saw and maps of how to get there. In both clearings, there were questions to think about and tales to unravel. Who used to come here, and for what reason? Were there ceremonies of any kind? Did anyone play games here?

It was obvious that these secret clearings stirred their imaginations. The clearings were endowed with a certain beauty and sense of mystery, and the campers enjoyed speculating about them and making up stories.

In a School Library Setting

Sixteen years later, working as a library media specialist, I returned to the theme of Secret Clearings after reading the Indian folktale *Once a Mouse* (Brown) to a group of third graders. This tale, set in a jungle clearing, is about an over-bearing tiger that is taught a lesson by a hermit with magical powers.

In the discussion that ensued, I asked the children to think about other secret clearings in other stories. For example, in a Grimm's fairy-tale forest, one might spy a gleeful Rumplestiltskin (Diamond) celebrating his trickery as he dances by a fire, or a phony, effusive hag sweet-talking two lost children to step inside her house (Marshall).

The following week, I introduced to them passages about clearings from three other books. In *A Winter Place* (Radin), a young girl describes a clearing hidden in the hills with a lake "icebound quiet," where townspeople go skating and ice fishing. Eleven-year-old Adam, in *The Cardboard Crown* (Bulla), uses his clearing as a refuge for being alone and thinking. Emily in *Emily and the Green Circle* (Kennedy) lives in a trailer and is always moving from place to place. Her newly discovered clearing represents permanence to her, and she yearns to settle there and experience a more stable life.

The children were then encouraged to describe, through writing, a clearing where they may have built a hideout, visited from time to time, or simply wandered into. Some chose instead to develop stories using a clearing as the setting.

....

Alone in a Clearing

I cannot find sticks to build my fire, and I don't know my way around. I keep hearing noises, and I don't know what they are. I feel so alone, so scared. I feel like a wolf is about to attack me. If I could just pass the night.... Now I have my fire set, but I keep seeing dead men and scary monsters in the flames. I reach into my pocket and pull out a rock, my lucky rock. I tell myself to calm down and just sleep.

David Kramer, age 8

....

In the third session, I read aloud *Owl Moon* (Yolen) and *The Man Who Could Call Down Owls* (Bunting). Both reveal moonlit clearings where people come to communicate with owls. The first is a lyrical treatment of a father and daughter's outing, and the second, a provocative fable about a man and his extraordinary gift. Inspired by these works, children tried to capture these two night scenes through drawings and paintings.

In the next few sessions, children divided into small groups, creating original plays about something strange or magical that one might see in a secret clearing. In their plays:

A pirate captures a feisty leprechaun to find out the location of the pot of gold.

A loyal squire tries to coax an old knight to get ready for his last tournament.

An old-fashioned girl, a fox, and the Queen Rabbit practice tricks for a magic show.

A goblin and his chatty assistant experiment with new recipes and ingredients as they prepare for their nightly feast.

Two tree fairies show off their new bells and wings at the annual forest fashion parade.

These improvised dramas were performed with charm and vitality. Children were deeply invested in this project because the plays had sprung forth from their imaginations. In later sessions, they made illustrated storybooks based on their plays, and with the art teacher, they created papier-mâché puppets of their character.

Later that spring, they presented their plays as puppet shows to an audience of younger children. This experience helped them to be confident and empowered. For eight weeks, they had played with the same theme without ever losing interest. They had taken one concept and brought it to life in three different forms (dramatic play, story writing, and puppet making).

It was exciting to see two groups of children embrace this theme in such different ways. Those at the camp had the actual physical experience of hiking, searching, and finding a clearing—using all of their senses. They could see the clearing, observe the space and shadows, smell the pines, and touch the natural contours of the environment they encountered.

In contrast, children in the library media center were involved in a journey that led them to find secret clearings in literature. They became absorbed in the images and stories the books presented.

These vivid literary experiences inspired the children to draw on their memories and empowered them to create unique clearings of their own. As literary explorers, they had also journeyed deeply and widely into their own imaginations, uncovering realms, sensations, and feelings that sought creative expression in many forms.

Secret Clearings are universal. They can be found almost anywhere. We happen upon them by accident, by design, through literature, or by following a guide. Anyone, at any time, might wander into a clearing and see a deer, catch a scent, or stop to inspect some ruins. Private and powerful, a clearing in whatever form is a place of wonder and reflection. As a theme, it cultivates a child's curiosity, enlarging that child's world.

THEME 2:
Turtles ·· ●

In a Camp Setting

Imagine the world from a turtle's point of view. Imagine moving that slowly. Imagine the things that might give you pleasure. Imagine the different parts of a day.

Another theme that emerged during my experience at sleepaway camp was the theme of Turtles. My particular group of campers enjoyed going on turtle hunts. In fact, at camp, a turtle was worth five or six frogs in terms of its trading value because turtles had shells, were harder to find, and were apt to live longer.

The children's favorite camp stories were about King Snapper, who ruled the lake and terrorized the fish. They also spent considerable time observing and playing with the bunk mascot, a tiny box turtle that was kept in a large plastic crate on the porch of the cabin.

It is easy to project human feelings onto a turtle, because turtles often seem to be deliberating, concentrating hard, and moving purposefully. This is perhaps why children are so intrigued by them.

They are fascinated by their lumbering style, by the way they carry their homes on their backs, by the designs and spots on their shells, and by both their anatomy and longevity. In practical terms, they are curious about how turtles survive from day to day, what they eat, how they deal with predators, and where they go when the weather turns nasty.

To tap further into their interest, each night I would tell them stories about turtles—a mixture of fables, folktales, and Native American myths. For our bunk project, these 10-year-olds decided to create their own turtle story and develop it into a play. We worked on this mostly during rest hour.

···

Up Went the Turtle (a Scenario)

Every afternoon, an old turtle would climb up the same imposing boulder. When he reached the top, he would stick his head far out of his shell, and then share all his thoughts and observations with the Sky God.

He would describe all the things he had seen that morning—perhaps an exquisitely designed spider's web, a squirrel's private stash of acorns, or a wren nursing a broken wing. Sometimes he would embellish an incident and turn it into a wonderful story.

Other creatures saw how hard the old turtle struggled to move his body, and wondered if his efforts were worth it. Why bother? Why go to all that trouble? Was the Sky God even listening?

On the old turtle's very last day on earth, once again he began his journey. But he was weak, his legs were in pain, and the boulder, on that day, was extra slippery after a night of pounding rain.

"Come and have a salad with me," said his friend the rabbit. "We'll eat crunchy carrots and radishes, and share special memories." The old turtle thanked him for his offer, but still headed on his way.

"Come and see my newest prize," insisted the crow. "I'll even show you my secret treasure spot. I think you'll be very impressed." The old turtle was touched by this, but knew he needed to continue.

"Come rest with me in the sun," encouraged the lizard. "We can stretch out and relax and feel all those delicious rays." This sounded rather delightful, but the old turtle was determined to begin his climb.

Finally, he reached the base of the boulder. Upward he went. The climbing was slow, and several times he almost lost his footing. Maybe the other animals were right. Maybe he was wasting his time.

The old turtle didn't make it to the top until nighttime, and then he was exhausted. He had used all his muscle and stamina to make the trip. Now, when he stretched his neck, it was incredibly sore. When he began to speak, he had no words.

All of a sudden, a powerful orange light illuminated the entire boulder. The old turtle heard a voice, a voice that echoed throughout the forest.

"Welcome, gentle Turtle, I've been waiting for you. I knew you would come, but now it is my turn to do the talking, and you can be the listener. I want to thank you for all the things I've learned from you. Each day, I looked forward to your stories. They were wise and funny and sweet, and I never was disappointed."

....

The inspiration for this play was the tiny box turtle living on the porch of the cabin. It seemed to the children that every afternoon, ritualistically, the turtle would climb up the big rock that had been placed inside and stretch out its neck, checking out the sun and the sky. To them, the turtle was trying to say something important.

It took several sessions to develop the story line and play. Why was the turtle always climbing the rock, and to whom was he trying to talk? These were the two questions that stimulated the children's thinking. One camper suggested that he might be trying to communicate with Mother Nature, the Spirit of the Forest, or the Sky God. Another had the idea that he made this same journey each afternoon, but not until his last day on earth did the Spirit speak back to him.

We spent considerable time discussing the character of the old turtle and how he was so steadfast and dedicated. A third camper introduced the idea of having some other animals in the play, friends of the turtle—maybe a rabbit, a lizard, and some kind of bird.

When these seven kids at last performed their play, they were totally convincing. Five played the different roles, and two were the narrators. Part of the magic was that they presented the play outside at night, using a real boulder.

Wearing simple costumes, they relied a lot on their voices and body movements, and all of their lines were improvised. To create the effect of the Sky God's light, they used a flashlight and orange cellophane. This was truly an organic and heartfelt play, the perfect play for a summer camp night.

In a Hospital Setting

For hospitalized children, being cut off from summertime pleasures can make them extremely sad. Instead of experiencing the joy and freedom that come with the season, they are coping with new kinds of foods, new rituals, new faces, and even a new vocabulary to learn—terms like ER, OR, ICU, and IV.

Many of these children may feel exposed and vulnerable, having to wear small white gowns and deal with constant assaults on their body. They are filled with apprehensions and concerns. "What is going to happen to me?" "Will I get well?" "Will I get the needle?" "Will the nurses be nice?" "When will my family visit me?" "What happens during the night?"

Naturally, at this time, the body is the source of much anxiety, for something is either broken or does not work right anymore, and its image can be badly distorted. A child must reconnect to it somehow and figure out ways to cope with discomfort, pain, and limited mobility.

Often during their stay, children feel a loss of spirit that comes from being cut off from all things important. They miss brothers and sisters and friends. They miss moving around and playing outside. They miss all the familiar patterns of their normal lives. Ultimately, they begin to feel bored, restless, frustrated, confined.

As one of two play therapists in a New York City hospital, I met regularly with a group of older children right after rest hour in the pediatric playroom. Here, they could complain, share their humor, and express whatever emotions they were feeling. Sometimes they liked to describe their nightmares and dreams.

....

I had a dream, a horrendous dream that three million needles were after me, and they were ready to attack. They had big[,] long[,] pointing heads and they were laughing.

Written by a hospitalized 12-year-old boy

....

In these sessions, children would often write poetry, compose music, or make clay figures. Such vehicles for self-expression helped them to confront their aloneness and work through their fears and outrage.

During one session in July, children shared what they missed about having to stay indoors. With wistful faces, they reminisced about swimming, waiting for the ice-cream man, playing ball, and, especially, going to the park.

For city children, the park is the center of summer life, a gathering spot for families, and a place with a myriad of activities and choices. Once inside, they can find shade and comfort, quietude and adventure, and there are usually others to hang out with.

In our discussion, children began to think about how important parks were and how they fulfilled so many needs. They thought, too, about how parks were designed and maintained.

Soon they began exchanging park tales—tales about getting lost in the thickets, discovering a giant rat, finding a ten-dollar bill, sailing a new boat in the sailboat pond, seeing bees raid a family picnic, sneaking into a concert at night, getting a kite tangled in a tree, and getting a famous actor's autograph.

Later, someone suggested that they transform the playroom into a summertime park. The idea caught on quickly, and the children began playing with what their park would offer and what roles they might assume. They were not sure if the idea was practical or even possible, but they had enormous conviction and enthusiasm.

In the next few weeks, these nine children, coping with chronic diseases and broken limbs, set about to create this world. In planning sessions, they divided the labor and figured out what resources were available. They knew the nutritionist could help if they wanted to provide some kind of refreshments. They knew that among the birthday materials in the playroom, they could find any balloons that they might need.

They also decided on their roles, choosing to be the mayor of the park, the tour guide, the juggler, the sketch artist, the photographer, the balloon man, and the ice-cream vendor. Two children chose to be actors, calling themselves The Park Bench Players. The props and costumes that children found and made helped to animate their characters.

During all of their free time, they focused on this project, constantly adding new details. Sometimes they would have to leave what they were doing to go for a treatment or take an X-ray, and some children had to maneuver around wearing braces and casts, sitting in wheelchairs, and walking with crutches.

When the playroom park opened at last on a Friday afternoon, they eagerly pulled in the younger children, parents, doctors, nurses, physical therapists, and custodians. Everyone was invited, and everyone came.

Vibrant and colorful and enhanced with murals of trees, this summertime world offered a pretend fishing pond, a paper-sculptured garden, a water table for trying out handmade sailboats, and a recreation area for playing checkers, dominos, and horseshoes. Visitors could also enjoy the tunes of a violin player (one of the fathers) or skits put on by the Park Bench Players (one skit involved a conflict between a wacky pigeon and the Queen of the Squirrels). The only activity that did not succeed was kite flying, and that was because the fan was not working.

On this special day, these children seemed confident and secure in their roles. They enjoyed playacting and loved welcoming the guests and showing them around. It was obvious that the grown-ups were impressed and delighted.

What a turnabout this was, for the medical staff had to depend on them to learn about the ways of the park, the rules, and the activities being offered. Now the children were the ones in charge, the ones with all the information.

Through this kind of experience, the creative process became a restorative process, an important way of healing. It enabled these children to fight back, feel powerful, and create something whole.

THEME 4:
Fairy Tales .... ●

In a Classroom Setting

....

In fairy tales, there's romance. There's comedy. There are things that will give you nightmares. And there are things that will keep you laughing for the rest of your life.

Genevieve Snow, age 8

....

An exploration of fairy tales lends itself to any type of setting. For children, fairy tales are like old friends and companions. They are concerned with dreams and yearnings, good and evil, and offer endless possibilities for dramatic play. They can be comforting, too, since they provide children with a sense of order and justice. Heroes and heroines triumph, and villains get their comeuppance.

Such an exploration can enable children to become immersed in the fairy-tale world and its faraway time and setting. After reading a number of these tales, they can begin to identify the common elements that link these stories together.

For example, the words "Once upon a time" and "Happily ever after" often serve to frame these tales. The main characters are likely to go on important journeys. They may live in oppressive families whose members treat them unfairly, even cruelly. They are usually exposed to some kind of peril in the outside world that may take the form of a revengeful queen or a menacing wolf. They may also encounter people with magical powers and otherworldly creatures such as mermaids, gnomes, giants, or elves.

Transformation, another key element in fairy tales, can be an intriguing plot device—a marionette becomes a real boy, a frog becomes a prince, a serpent becomes an African king. The villains with their brooding, calculating, poisonous ways help to create a sense of drama and doom. They are masters in the art of treachery who take pride in their clever ploys and disguises.

To culminate a study of fairy tales with third and fourth graders, the classroom teacher and I (as the resource specialist) had each child choose a character and develop a short monologue that would try to capture that character's worries, dreams, or point of view.

In their monologues, Rhodopis, the slave girl in *The Egyptian Cinderella* (Climo), expresses her sadness after a falcon stole one of her red-rose slippers. Now she wonders if she will ever feel like dancing again. The Emperor in *The Emperor's New Clothes* (Andersen) describes his moment of humiliation when he was first aware that he was parading naked before the crowd. How will he explain to his subjects why he was so foolish and gullible?

From *Theme Play: Exciting Young Imaginations* by Gary Zingher. Wesport, CT: Libraries Unlimited. Copyright © 2006.

The following are the monologues of Puss from *Puss in Boots* (Brown) and Jack from *Jack and the Beanstalk* (Kellogg):

....

I'm a remarkable cat, and I'm great at tricks. Catching rabbits is my specialty. I'm so smart that I can trick an ogre, and I even met the king.

Blair Brown, age 9

Oh, man, is life hard. My mom's going to hate me. This can't get any worse. I sold our cow for three measly beans. Oh, man, how cheap is that? The guy that I got the beans from said they were magic, and I actually believed him. When I held them in my hand, and said "abracadabra"—nothing happened. I must be the biggest fool in the world.

Grant Levine, age 9

....

Children next prepared for a special ceremony. Each of them created a pantomime, a prop, and a piece of advice, all relevant to their character and story. At the ceremony, they each presented these, one at a time, standing in the heart of our fairy-tale circle.

Examples of Fairy Tale Characters

Character	Pantomime	Prop	Piece of Advice
Puss	his encounter with the ogre	his bag for catching rabbits	"A clever lie can sometimes help you."
Jack	his first wondrous climb up the beanstalk	the giant's magic harp	"Always keep your axe nearby."
Renee from *Toads and Diamonds*	her bringing water from a spring for a pleasant old woman	some of the flowers and jewels that fell out of her mouth	"A little politeness can sure pay off."
Shang from *Lon Po Po*	her pulling the wolf in a basket halfway up the gingko tree, and then letting go	the basket	"Beware of grandmothers with thorns on their hands."

As part of the celebration, some of the children created a giant three-dimensional map of the fairy-tale kingdom and its castles, villages, and woods to serve as a backdrop. This map was very detailed, highlighting Hansel and Gretel's breadcrumb trail and the actual goodies in Little Red Riding Hood's basket. Among the scrumptious snacks served that day were Jack's magic bean soup and the Fairy Godmother's pumpkin cakes.

THEME 5:
Labyrinths ···●

In a Classroom Setting

···

A labyrinth is a huge maze full of tunnels and traps and mixed-up creatures and deadends.

Anna Minksy, age 11

In a labyrinth, you are confused. You feel scared because you wonder if you'll ever get out again. You take your time and try to remember which way you went. You wonder if there will be any wild animals. The walls seem to be closing in on you. They get closer and closer and closer. Then you look up and see a light. You've found the exit!

Marcus Boykin, age 11

I look around and see darkness. I look back and there is a path fading behind a mirror-like wall. I take a step and the floor seeps in like sand. I take another and it's hard as rock. I run, then I fall, losing memory of what just happened.

Aisa Yamaguchi, age 11

I interviewed my mother and she thinks a labyrinth is something confusing and hard to understand. I interviewed my brother and he thinks that a labyrinth involves someone who is on a journey, and is trying to get home.

Elvira Castillo, age 11

···

The reading aloud of *The House of Dies Drear* (Hamilton) triggered an exploration of the theme of Labyrinths. The fifth-grade teacher and I, as the library media specialist, guided this project.

In this novel, the labyrinth depicted is an old house with tunnels and passages linking the past and present with a haunting, riveting power. It is a house that once provided refuge for slaves and was part of the Underground Railroad.

One might say that to enter a labyrinth is like walking inside the heart of a riddle. It demands problem solving, making choices, and rethinking one's steps. The experience itself can be risk-taking and perilous, challenging and exhilarating. Older children can identify personally with this theme, because it addresses their fear of being separated, of losing direction and control.

In our discussions, we began to define the word and to consider a number of questions. Is a labyrinth a place or a state of mind? What are some of the labyrinths in history, such as the pyramids and catacombs? Who created the English garden hedges and topiaries? What buildings in this country are known for their architectural mazes (Grand Central Station, the Pentagon, the Winchester House of San Jose).

Other labyrinths that children identified were a termite city, an anthill, a molehill, the inner human brain, the city of Venice, a house of mirrors, the Phantom's Opera House, a conspiracy, a trial, and any Sherlock Holmes mystery. They began to see that the concept of the labyrinth could apply to a number of things. Why is it that investigative reporters are often lost in the labyrinth of information and false leads? What are the experiences of immigrants who feel vulnerable and disoriented having to deal with so much red tape, without knowing the dominant language?

They thought, too, about the labyrinths described in different chapter books. Protagonists often puzzle over which direction to move in as they seek their way out of the maze.

In *The Fellowship of the Ring* (Tolkien), Frodo and his companions go through Moria, the home of ancient dwarfs. It is a true labyrinth, and they almost do not get back.

The curious Alice in *Alice's Adventures in Wonderland* (Carroll) finds that things keep changing as she encounters all kinds of confusing characters in a magical and maddening world.

....

Alice falls into a rabbit hole, into a hall of doors, gets bigger and smaller, meets strange characters, gets in trouble, makes friends, and wakes up in a dream. She doesn't know where to go, what to say.

Renee Reynolds, age 11
....

Slake's Limbo (Holman) illustrates how a boy survives underground in the labyrinth of the New York City subway system.

....

For Slake, living in a train station is like being in a maze, because he doesn't know where he is going to go, or how he is going to end up next. He has to find his new home and different ways to get around.

Amanda Johnson, age 12
....

We next divided the class into research groups so they could find information about the labyrinth that most interested them, both in literature and in the real world. The Minotaur group studied Greek gods and then dramatized the myth of Theseus and the monster using narration, mime, masks, and drums. The *Alice in Wonderland* group learned about Lewis Carroll, the Victorian age, and the importance of good manners and then, through dramatic play, brought to life the Mad

Hatter's Tea Party. The Subway group investigated the problems entailed in building the subway and the problems existing today. They made model constructions of a subway car and a ghost station. The Castle and Dungeon group collected information about these fortresses and then created an elaborate map of a castle and its internal layout—including chambers, halls, floors, and any secret areas.

To culminate this research adventure, all of the students collaborated in transforming the classroom into a giant labyrinth made out of brown paper walls, boxes, and cardboard. Each group had its own section, and everyone chose to dress in costumes to surprise the younger children who would be coming to visit.

Naturally, construction problems loomed, and the classroom labyrinth took three full mornings to create. Children wondered if it would be sturdy enough or if it would keep falling down. They quickly learned how to reinforce materials and were often called upon to be scavengers and problem-solvers, architects and engineers.

Several of the children visited the first and second graders to prepare them for their trip to the labyrinth. They defined a labyrinth and gave them a preview of what they might see. Then, they had children create their own mazes, drawing them on large sheets of construction paper.

On the day the labyrinth came to life, the first and second graders entered the fifth-grade classroom both puzzled and excited. "What happened to the desks and chairs?" they wondered. "Where were all the books and supplies?" A child dressed as the Dormouse greeted them, explaining what to look for and reminding them to move in a careful manner.

Once inside, younger children could crawl through tunnels, exploring any of the different sections. Some could enjoy tea and riddles with Alice, the Mad Hatter, and the March Hare. Others could step into the dungeon of an English castle and listen to stories about knights or put a token in a subway token booth and visit an eerie ghost station no longer used. And those who dared could figure a way in and out of the Minotaur's Maze, peeking at this strange and fierce beast from a very safe distance.

....

I like the way the labyrinth turned out. Everyone was running around and laughing. Most of them thought it was real except for this one little girl who thought everything was fake. No matter what you said, she thought it was fake.

Marcus Boykin, age 11

When we started painting I thought, 'Oh, no, we're not going to be able to finish!' While we were hanging the paper and arranging desks, I thought about all the technical problems that could possibly happen. Desks falling down, kids too rough, paper falling, and a whole lot more. When it was all set up, I looked at it, and I thought it was great, and that it would work fine.

Beechie Kitzinger, age 11

....

The fifth graders who created the labyrinth could not really believe that they had pulled it off, transforming their classroom into such an extraordinary maze. The experience was so powerful that, years later, the older children were still talking about how they served real tea at Alice's party and how they used real "special effects" to bring the Minotaur to life. In Texas, people often say, "Remember the Alamo!" At our school, you might hear those immortal words, "Remember the Labyrinth!"

For the 6- and 7-year-olds, the experience introduced them to the idea of the labyrinth, and they began to understand its meaning. When they arrived, they were incredibly curious and loved the idea of crawling through tunnels and peering into certain passages. They wondered, with each turn, what surprises would be waiting for them, and this generated enormous suspense.

Working on this unit of study allowed me to collaborate with the classroom teacher, to pool our skills and resources, and attempt a project that was particularly ambitious. We were in this together, building our partnership, bouncing ideas around, often rethinking our plans. And except for the week of construction, we never got too overwhelmed.

The Relevance of Thematic Journeys

Whatever the setting, thematic journeys have a cumulative effect that deepens and enhances a child's sense of possibilities. They help children to find in themselves previously untapped resources that can enrich their sense of independence and purpose. Furthermore, they allow children to be collaborators, creators, and visionaries-in-training.

Over time, these experiences can help children prepare for living in a grown-up world. They become more flexible and adaptable and perhaps able to respond to what life presents with greater confidence and originality.

Resources

Books

Andersen, Hans Christian. *The Emperor's New Clothes*. Candlewick, 1997.
Baum, L. Frank. *The Wonderful Wizard of Oz*. Books of Wonder, 2000.
Berger, Terry. *Black Fairy Tales*. Atheneum, 1969.
Brown, Marcia. *Once a Mouse*. Scribner, 1961.
Brown, Marcia. *Puss in Boots*. Scribner, 1952.
Bulla, Clyde. *The Cardboard Crown*. Crowell, 1984.
Bunting, Eve. *The Man Who Could Call Down Owls*. Macmillan, 1984.
Carroll, Lewis. *Alice's Adventures in Wonderland*. Abrams, 1988.
Climo, Shirley. *The Egyptian Cinderella*. Harper, 1989.
Diamond, Donna. *Rumplestiltskin*. Holiday, 1983.
Gannett, Ruth. *The Dragons of Blueland*. Knopf, 1987.
Hamilton, Virginia. *The House of Dies Drear*. Macmillan, 1968.
Hartwick, Harry. *The Amazing Maze*. Dutton, 1969.
Holman, Felice. *Slake's Limbo*. Scribner, 1974.

Huck, Charlotte. *Toads and Diamonds*. Greenwillow, 1996.

Kellogg, Steven. *Jack and the Beanstalk*. HarperCollins, 1991.

Kennedy, Mary. *Emily and the Green Circle*. Scholastic, 1987.

Marshall, James. *Hansel and Gretel*. Penguin, 1994.

Radin, Ruth. *A Winter Place*. Little, 1982.

Tolkien, J.R.R. *The Fellowship of the Ring*. Ballantine, 1965.

Van Laan, Nancy. *Rainbow Crow*. Knopf, 1989.

Yolen, Jane. *Owl Moon*. Philomel, 1987.

Young, Ed. *Lon Po Po*. Philomel, 1989.

3

The Power and Magic of Entrances

The theme of Entrances illustrates how powerful and complex certain themes can be. It touches all aspects of a child's world, for it deals with beginnings and transitions and what a child might be expecting, fearing, or hoping for.

In children's fantasies, entrances can indeed loom large. Images of H. G. Wells's time machine, the sealed tomb of King Tut, or the metal gates of Jurassic Park can be tingling and enthralling—images to be played with and then pocketed away when they become too real and too stark.

This exploration should stimulate children to think about the entrances in their day-to-day lives—those that are concrete and those that are emotional and symbolic. It should also allow them to tap into the realm of secret and magical entrances—the ones found in books, films, and their own private dream places.

Considering the Theme

Entrances are openings—physical structures where stories and journeys often begin. They can be powerful and evocative, arousing one's curiosity or setting off one's anxieties and fears. What are children's emotional responses when they enter a particular place or world? What feelings envelop them? Is there a welcoming sense, a warmth, a coldness, an edge? As children enter a place, do they feel big and important or small and diminished? In the sometimes subtle language of entrances, does the message say, "Relax, be yourself, you will be listened to and cared for?" or, does the message say, "Be cautious, don't speak, don't touch anything"?

This theme is rich in terms of dramatic possibilities. There is the sense of anticipation—the promise of friendship, romance, peace, wisdom, or sanctuary. Do children enter a place with an open mind or with already fixed perceptions?

Do they seek to enter, or are they forced to enter? Do they stumble upon the entrance, or are they searching for it?

Entrances can be portals for change; passages to another stage in life. They may lead children to take risks, leap with their imaginations, struggle, move forward, be reflective, reach out to others and be touched in return.

Who may enter a place? Is it open to everyone? Are fees assessed? Are homeless people welcome? Are there gender and age stipulations? Must one take an entrance exam or pass a literacy test? Are passports or green cards required? Entrances may be inclusive or exclusive. A sign that reads "Whites Only" or "No Girls Allowed" can hurt or devastate those who are kept away. To enter a clubhouse, one may have to know a secret knock or password. Some entrances are not accessible to those who are physically challenged.

Among entrances that fascinate children are doorways and stairways, court-yards and lobbies, tunnels and drawbridges. Children, on field studies, might examine entrances to various buildings and structures. What kind of decorations do they see? Which of these might welcome strangers, and which are designed to ward off evil? What are gargoyles? What are longhouse clan emblems? Why do the Pennsylvania Dutch put hex signs on their barns? Why do Jews keep me-zuzahs on the right side of their doors (Chaiken)?

Entering Homes

Families decorate and personalize the entrances to their homes to express the ways that they feel unique and the ways they feel bonded with others. These symbols help define who they are, reflecting their interests, concerns, and world-views. All kinds of objects provide clues to a family's identity: welcome mats, doorknobs and doorknockers, amulets, horseshoes, children's art, and religious and holiday ornaments. The pineapple may be used as a sign of hospitality, the pumpkin as a symbol of the harvest. Both ribbons and flags can convey strong political statements or not.

Stoops and porches are transitional places where children can pause and shift gears before going inside. These concrete worlds also function as stages, forums, and centers of play where children can interact and build friendships. In the poem "Stoops" (Rosen), a young girl cherishes her special vantage point, the third step, where she can observe street games like double Dutch and stoopball. She even feels a sense of ownership. The Mexican American author of *Family Pictures* (Garza) describes her brightly lit front porch at night as a convivial world where her family delights in eating watermelon.

What are the rituals practiced by members of various cultures upon entering their homes or the dwellings of others? What rituals are considered signs of respect? The Cambodian wife in *Judge Rabbit and the Tree Spirit* (Spagnoli) wel-comes the tree spirit, disguised as her husband, by pouring water over his feet. In the West African tale *The Village of Round and Square Houses* (Grifalconi), the grandfather enters the round house first and sits on a wooden stool. Then the uncle follows and sits on a mat. Children might research such welcoming rituals as embracing, bowing, shaking hands, covering one's head, taking off one's hat, removing shoes, ringing a bell, saying a prayer, bringing flowers, or offering a gift. Where do these rituals come from, and how did they evolve?

Entering Schools

When children start school, they enter with a myriad of concerns. Will they feel safe and comfortable? Will they make connections with their peers? Will the teacher recognize their special qualities and talents? This experience of school can be enriching. It can enhance their self-esteem and excite them to be thinkers, readers, and creators. But if the environment is harsh and punitive or chaotic and impersonal, the experience for children can be harmful, even traumatic.

Many books describe a child's emotional entry into school, capturing its tone, texture, rituals, and rules. Jay, the barefoot explorer in *A Pocketful of Cricket* (Caudill), embraces each summer day with gusto as he searches for pocket treasures and animals. What will school mean to him? Will it confine his spirit? When he brings his new pet the first day, it becomes his transitional object–his link to the outdoors. How will the teacher react when his cricket "fiddles" and disrupts the whole class?

A second child, Ut, the Vietnamese girl in *Angel Child, Dragon Child* (Surat), also has a special object. It is a wooden matchbox that contains a photo of her mother in Vietnam. This box gives her a measure of hope and security. It helps her endure the teasing she receives for wearing pajama-like clothes and not understanding the language and customs. The stone-gate entrance to Ut's new school makes her feel cold and empty. However, the conflicts in both of these stories are resolved in a creative and sensitive manner.

Merlene, the heroine in *Not Separate, Not Equal* (Wilkinson), is one of six African American students who integrate an all-white high school in Georgia in the 1960s. She has to enter cautiously with her emotions closed and must be prepared for acts of violence. How does she deal with threats, both real and imagined? How does she interpret these events? How does she keep her composure intact when all eyes are focused on her, eyes that are hostile and glaring?

Entering Special Places

What are the special places that inspire children–places that touch their poetic and romantic sides and allow their imaginations to flourish? Simply approaching such a place can make their hearts beat faster, whether it be a sleepaway camp or park, museum or library, after-school art program or community garden. Sometimes children create their own worlds of play and make-believe, places they might call Terabithia, Egypt, or Roxaboxen.

For Eloise (Thompson), magic happens at the Plaza Hotel, a world populated with desk clerks, mail clerks, and bell captains. She is quite at home with the marble pillars and revolving doors and would gladly provide an intimate tour.

....

Hi! My name is Eloise. I am going to give you a tour of the Plaza Hotel. When you arrive, you may choose which door you can use, the regular door or the swivel door. When you come in, notice the fancy and beautiful lobby. Look at the famous paintings on the walls. Look at your reflection on the newly waxed floor. Note the finely dressed bell hops.

Alexis Dell Ray, age 10

....

Ben in *Ben's Trumpet* (Isadora) and Amanda in *The Palace of Stars* (Lakin) have special places where they are uplifted and transformed—places rich in music and atmosphere. Ben's place is a neighborhood jazz club, even though he is too young to enter inside, and Amanda's is an elegant movie house.

For some children, the world of live theater can be particularly thrilling. Musicals and plays have the power to enchant—to move audience members and challenge the actors and dancers who are waiting backstage.

....

I peeked out of the red plush curtain. People! People! People! I felt numb. What if I were to fall down? What if I made a wrong move? I tried to rehearse my part in my head. I go out, bourreeing on dainty toes. Then I would do an arabesque. Then I would go flying through the air on a grand jete. My mom would clap with tears in her eyes. My brother would cheer and whistle. My sister would grumble and be jealous. Then, all of a sudden, my solo music started. I ran out on my toes, and I stumbled.

Chloe Kitzinger, age 9

....

Entering Scary Places

Sometimes to get from one place to another, children have to go through a dark, dreaded place—an alley, a tunnel, a forest. Sometimes the nightmare place is very close by, as near as a child's closet or basement. Any of these places can become pervasive and trigger anxious moments. What will happen when one enters inside? Will the stillness erupt into sounds of horror? Why are the shadows whispering?

In *The Ghost-Eye Tree* (Martin), a young boy must pass a large, ominous tree in dark woods when he goes to get milk for his mother. He deals with his fear by tilting his hat a particular way to suggest a "tough-guy" persona. N'Tombi, the Zulu girl in *N'Tombi's Song* (Seed), is also afraid of the forest. She worries about the "monster that lives in the dark" waiting to devour its prey. She tries to overcome her fears by singing to herself and balancing a sugar packet on her head. The Panamanian boy in the short story "The Cave" (Carlson) finds an eerie mix of sounds and smells in the dreaded cellar of his father's store. Once inside, he encounters a spider, a rat, and a "cat with hypnotic eyes." This causes him to panic, and he falls, becoming enmeshed in wire.

Even carvings on doors and figures on buildings can evoke a queasy feeling or a feeling of terror in children. What mysteries might be harbored in an entrance or entranceway? Does the brass doorknob ever turn when no one is there? What is the mystery of the whistling gate? And who might know the gargoyle's secret?

....

"The day is foggy, better be careful," the doorman said. "You could trip and fall." Outside I stumbled. The fog was dense and thick, and I could only see a few feet in front of me. Then red eyes appeared from my building. They moved back and forth, confusing me with illusions. It made me feel dizzy.

Reece Robinson, age 9

....

The hospital can be a very scary place for children, who enter feeling powerless and vulnerable. They have to wear identification bracelets and small white gowns. Out of anxiety, questions arise: "What's happening to my body?" "Will I get the needle?" "Will the IV hurt?" "When am I going home?" In this white, clinical world, there are pungent smells, medical carts, day shifts and night shifts. The nurse's station is the vital hub, and the playroom can be a refuge and a healing place. Vera Williams's *Scooter* gives a lively and personal account of how one child perceives her visit to a hospital emergency room.

Sometimes because of changing political realities, children are uprooted and forced to go into bleak, confining worlds—worlds that they might not be able to leave or escape from. They enter with knotted feelings, overwhelmed and cut off, having left behind loved ones and prized possessions.

Seven-year-old Emi, in *The Bracelet* (Uchida), must now go to a Japanese internment camp located in a former racetrack. She and her family encounter armed guards at the gate, and then they are locked inside. Guard towers and barbed wire define their boundaries. Apartment #40, their new home, is a dank, dismal stable where there is still the smell of horses. How does Emi survive this ordeal, and what, if anything, eases her sorrow?

Hannah, the heroine in *The Devil's Arithmetic* (Yolen), is transported back in time to a Polish shtetl where she becomes Chaya and is abruptly taken to a Nazi death camp. She is forced to undress and walk naked and to submit to a freezing shower, a severe haircut, and a tattoo pen that sears her flesh. In this brutal world, the indignities and horrors never cease.

....

Entering Other Cultures

Things look very different here. There are carriages, and I wish I could see who is inside, probably very rich people. I see stands with food I have never seen before. I also don't understand what people are saying. It sounds like people dropping pebbles into the water.

Emma Butensky, age 9

....

Entering other cultures and absorbing so many images and pieces of information can be confusing and dizzying. For those uprooted, there is so much to sort out and make sense of. *Ellis Island: New Hope in a New Land* (Jacobs) documents the history of Ellis Island with striking black-and-white photographs, explaining why it came to be and why it was closed. It looks at steerage and describes the process immigrants went through in this "gateway to a new life." Who was admitted? Who was turned back? What diseases were doctors looking for?

In more personal terms, the story of Fanny, an 8-year-old from Russia, is rendered in *Gooseberries to Oranges* (Cohen). She feels lonely in Ellis Island, a small girl in a huge room, who does not know the language. The book is vivid and detailed in capturing Fanny's first impressions of a crowded New York City: "clothes on fire escapes, cats, peddlers, rotting apples and garbage, huge barrels of newspaper."

Another young immigrant is Moon Shadow, the hero in *Dragonwings* (Yep). He enters the United States from China, and his waiting place is a two-story warehouse. He emphatically does not trust the "custom demons," for he fears they will trick him and prevent him from being with his father. This San Francisco is not the Promised Land he had imagined. There are no "mountains of glittering gold," and the pale-colored box houses have no courtyards.

....

Entering Fantasy Worlds

To get to Elf City you might think you fly to the North Pole. Well, you are wrong. You simply walk to your mirror and say, "Muffle, Puffle!" Then the Grand High Elf greets you and takes your hat.

Reece Robinson, age 9

You can only enter this land while you are asleep. It seems like a dream but it is not. You are in the land of the fairies! You will dance and play with the fairies all night, but when morning comes you end up back in your bed. Sometimes you may find a little gift a fairy left for you like a bell flower that rings.

Julia Chmielowska, age 8

....

Secret worlds abound in children's fantasy books—worlds such as Oz (Baum), Narnia (Lewis), Blueland (Gannett), and MiddleEarth (Tolkien). These are unique, self-contained realms that readers and dreamers are permitted to enter and travel through. A strong ethical core anchors each of these books—one that ensures order, resolution, and justice. Yet the journeys are still marked with surprises and ironies, bizarre encounter, and breathtaking detours. Often in these stories, there is a balance of nonsense and reason, generosity and treachery.

Entrances to imaginary worlds can be quite diverse. They can look puzzling or ordinary and may take the form of a tollbooth, wardrobe, tunnel, or looking glass. These devices are essential, for they set the story in motion. They offer a prelude to the journey, a taste of what is to come.

....

The garden door was really mysterious. It was a double door that was slightly opened, and I could see the mist on the ground seeping through the crack. Only the door stood between reality and mystery.

Jonathan Gillam, age 10

....

Who are the travelers who dare to enter, and once they go inside, how will they be changed? The heroes and heroines who journey into make-believe lands learn to be clever and resourceful as they go on quests, solve riddles, and deal with the unexpected and the unknown. They may even begin to discover new dimensions in themselves and to rethink their universe.

Grand Entrances

What are grand entrances? Most individuals enter a place quietly, unnoticed and unheralded. But some may enter dramatically with spotlights and drumrolls, fanfare and flourishes. Think of Peter Pan's first stage entrance, Eliza Doolittle being announced at the ball, the bullfighter stepping into the ring, the home team in baseball taking the field.

Imagine an elephant walking up the steps and through the open doors of a cathedral followed by a llama, a camel, and an entire procession of pets. This joyful event happens yearly at St. John the Divine's in New York City to honor St. Francis of Assisi, the patron saint of animals.

Sometimes, though, grand-scaled entrances can go awry and amiss. Two characters in picture books turn things around so that possible fiascos instead become important triumphs. In *Mirette on the High Wire* (McCully), Mirette, a girl in Paris, offers support to the fear-struck Bellini so that he can continue with his act. In *Lentil* (McCloskey), a boy in Ohio saves the day with his harmonica, much to the chagrin of Old Sneep, the town character whose lemon slurps have unnerved the Alto town band.

Playing with the Theme

How can children be encouraged to tap into the richness of the theme? What kinds of projects might engage them? Would they want to pursue an aspect of the theme on their own, with a partner, or in a group?

Just think about the possibilities. Younger children might want to make up their own "knock knock" jokes, read and dramatize *Who's in Rabbit's House?* (Aardema), or create musical entrances for all the characters in *The Camel Who Took a Walk* (Tworkin).

Middle-grade children could create their own passwords and secret knocks, design the entrance to a funhouse, or develop an entrance exam for Hogwarts Academy.

Older children could write journal entries from the point of view of one of the stone lions guarding the New York City Library or investigate the rites of passage in various cultures (the bar mitzvah, the Aboriginal walkabout, the Hindu Upanayana). Some could explore the idea of entering contests and interview grandparents and other adults about old radio contests and dance marathons of the 1930s and 1940s.

The following activities invite children to play with the theme of Entrances, using their poetic and expressive sides to explore its many facets. Excursions are suggested in the areas of art, storytelling, dramatic play, and creative writing.

Art Excursions

Mirror Drawings.   Anthony Browne's *Through the Magic Mirror* could inspire younger children to create drawings about what they might see if they entered a land of opposites and oddities. Perhaps a juggler would be juggling only one ball, or a rabbit would be pulling a man out of a hat. The author's haunting story *The Tunnel* could stimulate other kinds of drawings. What would it feel like to walk through this tunnel, and what might one discover on the other side?

Shoebox Worlds.   Children could create peep worlds or dioramas of places they imagine or places from favorite books. These worlds might have special doors, gates, or peepholes. By just peeking inside, one could enter Strega Nona's kitchen, the Secret Garden, the Hall of the Mountain King, a Persian marketplace, or the Forest Primeval.

Sky Murals.   Children could paint a giant mural showing the ways characters from folktales enter the sky world. The mural might depict Jack climbing the beanstalk and Ananse, the Spider Man, spinning his web. Other ways of reaching the sky are described in such Native American tales as *Arrow to the Sun* (McDermott), *Ladder to the Sky* (Esbensen), and *A Boat Ride with Lillian Two Blossom* (Polacco).

Model Entrances.   Working in small groups, middle-grade and older children could create three-dimensional models of the entrances to the secret worlds in fantasy books. First, they should carefully read and reread passages describing their entrance, focusing on the details. What makes it unique and distinctive? The wardrobe of Narnia (Lewis), for example, has a furry texture and perhaps the scent of mothballs. The tunnel into the Giant Peach (Dahl) has sweet juicy drippings coming from the walls. Children could design their entrances through a series of drawings and then create them out of wire and papier-mâché. An exhibit of their entrances might include the rabbit hole that leads to Wonderland, the Phantom Tollbooth, and the gate to Emerald City. This project was originally suggested in *At the Pirate Academy: Adventures with Language in the Library Media Center* (Zingher).

Storytelling Excursions

Key Tales. Many evocative picture books can be used to stimulate children to make up and tell their own stories. In *This Is the Key to the Kingdom* (Alison), unlocked doors invite a girl and her dog into a caressing, dreamlike world where there are games, treats, and wonderful sights. Is this world real or a fantasy? Who is the man with the flute sitting near the gate, and who is the loving woman inside? After some discussion, children can each pull a key from a jar, making up a story about the door it unlocks and the adventures that unfold. Another possibility is to pass the same key from child to child, so each has a turn, adding to a story-in-the-round.

Greek Myths. Middle-grade or older children might share stories from Greek myths, in which entrances are pivotal to the plot. What happens when Theseus enters the maze of the Minotaur's den? What was Odysseus's clever plan to enter the walled city of Troy? What happens to Odysseus and his men when they enter the cave of Polyphemus, the Cyclops? An excellent sourcebook is *Greek Myths* (McCaughrean).

Heroic Jewish Figures. Another story-sharing session might highlight some of the dramatic episodes in Jewish history. What happens when David enters the valley to combat Goliath, when Daniel enters the lion's den, when Jonah enters the whale? What are the consequences when Esther enters the King's chamber and reveals her identity? In the story of Passover, why did the Jews put blood on their doorposts? Why on Seder nights is the door left open for Elijah?

Junk Worlds. The magic of "junk" will become clear to children as they build miniature worlds, in small groups, with bags of assorted objects (seashells, spools, clothespins, watch parts, thimbles, batteries, buttons, spools, cork, ribbon, fabric, funnels, pieces of mirror and driftwood). Each group, using all of their objects, must also create an entrance to their world and a story that takes place there. A pipe-cleaner hoop might serve as an entrance to a flea circus, or a wall of shells could mark the beginning of an undersea paradise. After a twenty-minute work session, everyone could travel from world to world, with each group pointing out their entrance, describing what they have built, and, finally, sharing their story (Zingher).

Dramatic Play Excursions

Who Is Knocking? Younger children could become characters from folk and fairy tales and create improvisations about who is knocking at the door. Could it be Lon Po Po, the Dream Stealer, or a craggy-faced lady with an apple? A perfect sourcebook is George Shannon's *A Knock at the Door*. Each tale presented here involves a knocker, who pretends to be someone else and plans to do great harm. The character or characters inside must outwit the intruder. This multicultural collection includes such stories as "Grandmother and the Apes" from Uganda and "Los Seis Cabritos" from Mexico.

Encounters at the Gate. Middle-grade or older children, working in pairs, might develop improvised mini-dramas that take place at the entrance to an imaginary palace. The royal gatekeeper, weary but patient, must keep the peace and monitor who goes inside. What if a visitor does not know the password or have a document with the royal seal? What are the gatekeeper's best and worst moments? Who might he or she have to contend with during the course of a day? Some possibilities:

- A beggar who is always spouting off about the days when people were more generous.
- A pushy merchant who has invented an all-purpose polish.
- The town sweeper who is appalled by any kind of litter.
- The gatekeeper-in-training who is extremely eager to learn the ropes.

In the Future. Episodes of *The Twilight Zone* (Zicree) might be shown to older children to excite their imaginations about time travel, other dimensions, and futuristic worlds. In the year 2050, will the world seem hopeful and humane, or cold and antiseptic? What institutions might exist to meet the needs of society? What are the stories of people waiting in line to enter the Antique Auction, Coupon Redemption House, Emotion Center, Truth Court, and Ten-Minute Park? Children could develop their ideas first through writing. Then, in small groups, they could create original plays.

....

The police woman pushed open the door of the Truth Court. I heard drums. I knew they were in my imagination, but I heard them still. Slowly, I walked in the court, using the drum beats to set my pace. I walked until I came to a bench with my name engraved on it. I had told a lie. I hope they hadn't figured it out.

Ariadne Emmanuel, age 12

I stood near the wall peeking through the tiny hole. I was trying to see the Ten-Minute Park. People say you could take your gas mask off and run free in there. I had been told of colors, bright and beautiful, of lovely breezes and tiny, flickering lights that came out of the dark and flew about. I waited for my chance to sneak in.

Lily Thom, age 11

....

Creative Writing Excursions

Stoop Talk. Children might write poems or short dialogues that capture "stoop talk" or "porch patter." When eavesdropping, what is the content of the conversations they hear? Are there dialogues about who likes whom and about who got reprimanded at school? Or is the stoop talk about bottle caps and trading cards, alligators in the sewer, and creatures in the alleyway?

Fantasy Places. Children might describe what they see, hear, and smell when they first enter such imaginary places as Elf Alley, the Ghost's Garden, the Monkey's Palace, Time Town, the Whisper Station, the Beastie's Lair, or the Carnival of Colors.

....

In the Ghost's Garden, I can see dogs fishing in the Lake of Doom, and snakes eating eggs. There is a ghost band, and one ghost is playing the fiddle, and another is banging the drum.

Carlos Ortiz, age 8

I was waiting to enter Time Town, where time did not matter. I was scared, lonely, but most of all excited. I was at the Whisper Station when the Time Train arrived. I stepped aboard this magical train. It started moving faster, faster, faster. Splotches of color and clocks jumped out at me.

Gina Eichenbaum-Pikser, age 10

A small elf leads me through a dark passage dimly lit by candles. I look around, and it seems that I am in a mining tunnel. Far ahead, I see a bright yellowish glow. Suddenly, the bright glow is very near, and I enter Time Town, where the people live in clocks.

Erica Ciporen, age 10

....

The Inscription. Signs and inscriptions found at the entrance of a place can be telling or misleading, welcoming or intimidating. Older children might create the beginnings of stories where there is an entrance with a strong aura or mood, and an inscription that offers a mysterious clue. It might be the entrance to a cave or burial ground, schoolyard or park.

....

The gate was crumbling. Hanging from it was a sign, "Smell the flowers of education." Beyond the gate was an old, abandoned, broken-down school. Surrounding the school was a garden that may have once been beautiful. You could almost smell the roses.

Gina Eichenbaum-Pikser, age 10

An illustration of an imaginary world, Elf Alley. By Paul Kuemmerlein, age 13.

The inscription read "Henry D. Robbins National Park." Underneath was a strange message. "In memory of Henry D. Robbins who lost his life on these ———— slopes." The word between "these" and "slopes" was scratched off, illegible. There was a strange sense of mystery about the plaque. But ahead stood the trees, serene and peaceful.

Sasha Freudenberg-Chavkin, age 10

Resources

Books

Aardema, Verna. *Who's in Rabbit's House?* Dial, 1977.

Alison, Diane. *This Is the Key to the Kingdom.* Little, 1992.

Babbitt, Natalie. *Goody Hall.* Farrar, 1971.

Baum, L. Frank. *The Wonderful Wizard of Oz.* Books of Wonder, 2000.

Browne, Anthony. *Through the Magic Mirror.* Greenwillow, 1992.

Browne, Anthony. *The Tunnel.* Random, 1990.

Cameron, Eleanor. *The Wonderful Flight to Mushroom Planet.* Little, 1954.

Carlson, Lori. "The Cave," in *Where Angels Glide at Dawn.* Lippincott, 1990.

Carroll, Lewis. *Alice's Adventures in Wonderland.* Holt, 1985.

Caudill, Rebecca. *A Pocketful of Cricket.* Holt, 1964.

Chaiken, Miriam. *Menorahs, Mezuzas, and Other Jewish Symbols.* Clarion, 1990.

Cohen, Barbara. *Gooseberries to Oranges.* Lothrop, 1982.

Cohen, Barbara. *King of the Seventh Grade.* Lothrop, 1982.

Cole, Joanna. *Bony-Legs.* Macmillan, 1984.

Cole, Joanna. The Magic School Bus series. Scholastic.

Dahl, Roald. *Charlie and the Chocolate Factory.* Knopf, 1964.

Dahl, Roald. *James and the Giant Peach.* Knopf, 1961.

De Angeli, Marguerite. *The Door in the Wall.* Doubleday, 1989.

De Paola, Tomie. *Strega Nona.* Simon, 1979.

Esbensen, Barbara. *Ladder to the Sky.* Little, 1989.

Fast, Howard. *Tony and the Wonderful Door.* Knopf, 1968.

Gannett, Ruth. *The Dragons of Blueland.* Knopf, 1987.

Garza, Carmen. *Family Pictures.* Children's Book Press, 1991.

Grifalconi, Ann. *The Village of Round and Square Houses.* Little, 1986.

Hale, Edward. *The Man without a Country and Other Stories.* Airmont, 1988.

Haley, Gail. *A Story! A Story!* Atheneum, 1970.

Hamilton, Virginia. *The House of Dies Drear.* Macmillan, 1984.

Hamilton, Virginia. *The Planet of Junior Brown.* Macmillan, 1971.

Holm, Ann. *North to Freedom.* Peter Smith, 1984.

Holman, Warwick. *Theseus and the Minotaur.* McElderry, 1989.

Isadora, Rachel. *Ben's Trumpet.* Greenwillow, 1979.

Jacobs, William. *Ellis Island: New Hope in a New Land.* Scribner, 1990.

James, Betsy. *The Dream Stair.* Harper, 1990.

Juster, Norton. *The Phantom Tollbooth.* Knopf, 1961.

Kellogg, Steven. *Jack and the Beanstalk.* Morrow, 1991.

Lakin, Patricia. *The Palace of Stars.* Tambourine, 1993.

Lewis, C. S. *The Lion, the Witch, and the Wardrobe.* Macmillan, 1988.

Lindbergh, Anne. *Travel Far, Pay No Fare.* Harper, 1992.

Martin, Jr., Bill. *The Ghost-Eye Tree.* Holt, 1988.

McCaughrean, Geraldine. *Greek Myths.* McElderry, 1993.

McCloskey, Robert. *Lentil.* Viking, 1940.

McCully, Emily. *Mirette on the High Wire.* Putnam, 1992.

McDermott, Gerald. *Arrow to the Sun.* Viking, 1974.

McMullan, Kate. *The Great Ideas of Lila Fenwick.* Dial, 1986.

Naidoo, Beverley. *Journey to Jo'burg*. Lippincott, 1985.

Norton, Mary. *The Borrowers*. Harcourt, 1953.

Peters, Julie. *The Stinky Sneakers Contest*. Little, 1992.

Phillips, Mildred. *The Sign in Mendel's Window*. Macmillan, 1985.

Pinkwater, Daniel. *Lizard Music*. Putnam, 1976.

Pinkwater, Daniel. *Wingman*. Dodd, 1973.

Polacco, Patricia. *A Boat Ride with Lillian Two Blossom*. Philomel, 1988.

Rosen, Michael. *Home*. Sagebrush, 1996.

Seed, Jenny. *N'Tombi's Song*. Beacon, 1989.

Sendak, Maurice. *Where the Wild Things Are*. Harper, 1988.

Shannon, George. *A Knock at the Door*. Oryx, 1992.

Sharmat, Marjorie. *Gila Monsters Meet You at the Airport*. Macmillan, 1980.

Snyder, Zilpha. *Below the Root*. Atheneum, 1975.

Snyder, Zilpha. *The Egypt Game*. Atheneum, 1967.

Spagnoli, Cathy. *Judge Rabbit and the Tree Spirit: A Folktale from Cambodia*. Children's Book Press, 1991.

Staples, Suzanne. *Shabanu, Daughter of the Wind*. Knopf, 1989.

Steig, William. *The Real Thief*. Farrar, 1976.

Surat, Michele. *Angel Child, Dragon Child*. Raintree, 1983.

Thompson, Kay. *Eloise*. Simon, 1955.

Tolkien, J.R.R. *The Lord of the Rings*. HarperCollins, 2002.

Twain, Mark. *The Celebrated Jumping Frog of Calaveras County*. Creative Education, 1990.

Tworkin, Jack. *The Camel Who Took a Walk*. Dutton, 1974.

Uchida, Yoshika. *The Bracelet*. Philomel, 1993.

Wartski, Maureen. *A Boat to Nowhere*. Westminster, 1980.

White, E. B. *Charlotte's Web*. Harper, 1952.

Wilkinson, Brenda. *Not Separate, Not Equal*. Harper, 1987.

Williams, Vera. *Scooter*. Greenwillow, 1993.

Winthrop, Elizabeth. *The Castle in the Attic*. Holiday, 1985.

Yep, Laurence. *Dragonwings*. Harper, 1978.

Yolen, Jane. *The Devil's Arithmetic*. Viking, 1988.

Yolen, Jane. *Encounter*. Harcourt, 1992.

Zhitkov, Boris. *How I Hunted the Little People*. Dodd, 1979.

Zicree, Marc. *The Twilight Zone Companion*. Silman, 1992.

Zingher, Gary. *At the Pirate Academy: Adventures with Language in the Library Media Center*. American Library Association, 1990.

Films, Videos, and DVDs

The Dark Crystal, directed by Jim Henson and Frank Oz. Universal, 1982. 93 minutes.

The Day the Earth Stood Still, directed by Robert Wise. Fox, 1951. 92 minutes.

He Makes Me Feel Like Dancin'. Direct Cinema, 1984. 51 minutes.

In the Land Where Pirates Sing. Phoenix Films, 1980. 29 minutes.

Journey to the Center of the Earth, directed by Henry Levin. Fox, 1959. 129 minutes.

My Bodyguard, directed by Tony Bill. Fox, 1980. 96 minutes.

My Life as a Dog, directed by Lasse Hallstrom. Sweden, 1985. 100 minutes.

The Neverending Story, directed by Wolfgang Peterson. German/Britain, 1984. 94 minutes.

Sounder, directed by Martin Ritt. Fox, 1972. 105 minutes.

Stand by Me, directed by Rob Reiner. Columbia, 1986. 87 minutes.

Sugar Cane Alley, directed by Euzhan Palcy. France, 1984. 103 minutes.

The Twilight Zone-Collection 1, directed by Jos Addis and William Asher. CBS, 1959. 25 minute episodes.

Where the Wild Things Are. Weston Woods, 1973. 8 minutes.

4

The Child as Everyday Explorer

This chapter identifies some of the powerful themes of childhood, examining why they are so timeless and relevant. It looks at the questions these themes provoke and suggests books and films that would illustrate each theme. At the end of each exploration, ideas are presented for extending these themes in imaginative ways.

All of these themes provide content for developing programs and should be played with, nurtured, and expanded upon. There is no step-by-step formula or specific sequence of activities to follow, but the excitement of children and the questions they raise can help guide practitioners as they begin shaping their journeys.

What are a child's favorite parts of the day? Where would a child choose to go adventuring? What might a child discover along the way?

Children enjoy exploring their orbit of home and neighborhood when they feel safe and protected and know they have grown-ups to rely on. They are comforted by the rituals of the day, whether helping set the breakfast table or listening to pirate stories at night in bed. They are beginning to discover their interests and dimensions, and as they respond to physical and intellectual challenges, they achieve a measure of autonomy. This makes it easier for them to navigate in the world.

At all times, they are absorbing and taking in, interpreting and incorporating whatever they see and learn. They are eager to explore everything—their backyard, the local park, the public library, the firehouse, and they are fascinated by all types of pets and interesting people. This is their time for pretending and playacting, for creating and re-creating worlds, and for experimenting and asking important questions.

As children grow older, they still love to explore, but their concerns become more social. They may deeply want to connect to others their own age, to have a best friend or be part of a group. They want to understand why people behave in certain ways and may wonder why there are so many conflicts in the world. Their questions grow more complex, and the answers they find are not always satisfying.

Themes to Consider

Theme 1	A Morning Collage
Theme 2	Safe and Special Places
Theme 3	Treasures
Theme 4	Imagining and Pretending
Theme 5	Neighborhood Jams
Theme 6	The Movies
Theme 7	When Trouble Comes
Theme 8	Rain, River, and Sea
Theme 9	Oddballs
Theme 10	Bedtime Rituals and Nighttime Journeys

THEME 1:
A Morning Collage··· ●

Something draws a small boy out of bed, out of his house, and away from his yard. As he rushes to the top of a hill, he is lured by an enveloping yellow—a safe and magical light. He has come to witness the dawn. (*Wake Up, Jeremiah*, Himler)

A mother and her two children eat an early breakfast and then snuggle together on the family sofa. This is their hour of transition—the children's school day ahead; the mother's factory shift now over. It is the not the ideal meeting time, but they make the best of it, exchanging thoughts and waiting for the "pinkish gold sunrise." (*By the Dawn's Early Light*, Ackerman)

A bruised and dispirited boy, a runaway from a concentration camp, wakes up from his first uninterrupted sleep. When he looks down from his mountain, he is overwhelmed by the breathtaking vista below. The deep, vibrant colors are new to him—the dazzling reds and various shades of green, and "over all shone the warming sun not white-hot and spiteful and scorching, as the sun had shone upon the camp in the summertime, but with a warm, golden loveliness." Aroused by such beauty, he begins to feel tears. (*North to Freedom*, Holm)

With what fantasies, hopes, and uncertainties might children enter the day? What are the character and mood of a particular morning? What are its unique qualities? Is it gentle, raging, solemn, sparkling, windy, apple-flavored, pine-fla- vored, slushy, minty, smoky, fiery orange, or misty green? Is it a school day or a free day? Is it a morning for leaping up and trekking out or for nestling under covers, hibernating, and half-dreaming?

Some children wake up early to celebrate the break of day. They praise and embrace the sun through music and dance, meditation and prayer. *The Way to Start a Day* (Baylor) describes welcoming rituals throughout the world and such special offerings as feathers, gold, and marigolds, Aztec flute songs and Chinese bell songs. "A morning needs to be sung to. A new day needs to be honored." Some individuals make up their own songs and create their own cer- emonies.

If a child wakes up early enough, that child will be treated to a special time of day with a special light and stillness and a chance to begin the day clearheaded. Often, members of the Early Risers Club adventure in pairs. In *Dawn* (Shulevitz), an old man and his grandson, after camping out, greet the morning sun in the middle of a lake and feel a remarkable sense of calm. As the sun rises, they take in the subtle changes and quiet movements until, all at once, there is an abundance of light and color.

A mother and daughter enjoy a poetic outing in *Fog Drift Morning* (Ray) as they collect blueberries on top of a hill not far from shore. There is much to discover—to touch and to smell: "seaweed strains, sponge and kelp," "a handful of winkies," and " a perfect sand dollar."

From *Theme Play: Exciting Young Imaginations* by Gary Zingher. Wesport, CT: Libraries Unlimited. Copyright © 2006.

In *Good Morning, River!* (Peters), an old man, Carl, shares his secrets about the river with his young friend Katherine on their morning walks throughout the seasons. They observe the dark ice of the winter river and the river in spring "swollen with snow melt and rain." He has wisdom to impart, and she begins to share his passion, to read the signs, and understand what the river has to say.

Morning Girl (Dorris) is about a 12-year-old Taino child living on an island in pre-Columbian America. Her mother thinks she wakes up at dawn because she "dreams too hard" and "can't relax even in sleep." But Morning Girl loves the privacy and tranquility offered by these moments—the freedom to take in the beach, taste a mango, or even make blossom jewelry.

In *Maniac Magee* (Spinelli), a homeless boy sees these "appleskin hours" as his special time of day—a time when he can wander freely the avenues and alleyways. In these moments before the alarm clocks sound, he does not feel left out or disconnected. Instead, he experiences a sense of ownership, as though the morning and the town "all belonged to him" and "that he would be welcome anywhere."

In *The Castle Builder* (Nolan), a boy on a beach creates an elaborate castle with imagination, energy, and intense concentration. His labor of love is a spectacular fortress with formidable walls, windows, high towers, and an open courtyard. With his pocket hero, a plastic toy figure, he acts out scenarios in the sand, and his fantasy play sustains him throughout the morning. He imagines his Sir Christopher under siege, fending off evil knights and a dragon. But what happens when the morning tides begin to rise and surge, with waves crashing down on his kingdom?

Morning Feelings

What are the feelings of children when they first wake up? What are their needs, and will their needs be satisfied? Will they find nourishment, quietude, and affection? Will they have time for both private play and social engagement?

On some mornings, children would prefer to stay in bed, holding on to a sweet dream and letting it linger. But often, there may be joyful reasons for getting up and seizing the day—mornings with wonderful promise. They may anticipate visiting a parent's workplace, checking on newborn kittens, releasing butterflies in the meadow, frolicking in the first snow of winter, peeking under the pillow to see if the tooth fairy came, wearing a new jacket outdoors, having a play date with a good friend, or being the line leader at school.

The excited Maria in *Dumpling Soup* (Rattigan), who lives in Hawaii, cannot begin to contain her joy. She is the first one up on New Year's Eve day, and she cannot wait to see her cousins and to learn to wrap dumplings.

In *Willie Bear* (Kantrowitz) a young boy starting school for the first time musters courage and confidence by preparing his stuffed animal for this new venture. "Have you brushed your teeth? Have you washed your face?" Projecting his concerns onto Willie Bear helps him to cope with this dramatic change in his life.

Christopher, the young hero in *Sleep Out* (Carrick and Carrick), awakens with a sense of autonomy and pride. He has slept out by himself, and despite a few scares and hunger pains, he has survived the night intact and can now savor his feeling of euphoria.

Elliott in the film *E.T.* and Omri in *The Indian in the Cupboard* (Banks) both wake up with a secret knowledge and cannot wait to tap into the possibilities of the morning. For each, the day will allow them to become teachers and protectors. For each, an unusual friendship will begin to take root.

The young girl in *Up in the Mountains* (Lewis), on a morning almost a hundred years ago, cannot quite believe the news she is hearing. "You have a baby sister!" This is "jumping up" and "shouting" news when you already have three brothers.

But sometimes children awake with empty feelings and may carry their sadness through the entire day. If they leave home with their needs unmet, they may feel unsettled or angry.

In certain families, mornings have a rushed quality or a definite edge. Arguments may erupt at the breakfast table, and there may not be enough cereal or milk. Some children may withdraw emotionally in reaction to parents who are preoccupied or distant. The jarring sound of an alarm clock or the unrelenting cry of a baby may set a shrill and unpleasant tone.

Perhaps all children wake up at times with anxieties and fears. They may worry about not having enough money for lunch or a class trip. They may worry about what might happen if their parents separate, or if one of their parents is laid off from work. They may be anxious about school matters—report cards and spelling tests. What if they are called upon and unprepared?

Children are likely to have strong social agendas and can be quite troubled if there is a tear in a friendship or some type of misunderstanding. Some children may be fearful of a neighborhood bully or overwhelmed if someone they love is ill or dying. Some may feel embarrassed after wetting the bed on a sleepover or awkward waking up in an unfamiliar place like a hospital or shelter. The quality of their sleep can also affect their morning. To have a bad dream or restless night or to be awakened abruptly can make children feel fragile and unhinged.

Dawn, in *Dawn and the Round-to-It* (Smalls), feels lonely and ignored. Her need is to play and share and to be listened to; but everyone else just wants to sleep, and when they do get up, they are busy and often grouchy. How is she able to express her frustration creatively, and how does her family respond?

J.T., in the film *J.T.*, has an especially hard time in the morning. He dislikes getting out of bed and going to the bathroom in the hall. He hates being told by his mother how he is such a failure. His mornings are cold and joyless, almost without hope, but a one-eyed, battle-scarred cat may soon change all of that.

Little Eight John (Wahl), ever defiant, makes the mistake of sleeping with his head at the foot of the bed, and the next morning his superstitious family goes broke. Will this mean-spirited and exasperating boy finally learn to heed his mother's warnings? The title character in *Alexander and the Terrible, Horrible, No Good, Very Bad Day* (Viorst) starts his morning on the wrong foot, and his day becomes a disaster—a day of slights and injustices in which everything bad is personalized. Maybe he should just move to Australia.

On an early December morning, Sam Gribley, the young survivalist living on his own in *My Side of the Mountain* (George), must confront his fear of the approaching winter. The signs are clear—"the sudden chill," "the blackened sky," "the silent woodpeckers." It seems that the "dark clouds of winter" have begun to prevail, and now he must summon his strength and resources in order to stay sane and keep his bearings.

The uprooted Yuki in *Journey to Topaz* (Uchida) wakes up to sounds of hammering on her first morning in a Japanese internment camp. She is disoriented and not sure of the routines. Her new home is a horse stall. The mattresses are scratchy, and there are no doors on the latrines. Will she ever again know comfort and privacy?

Anne Frank experiences her mornings in hiding. She must at times hold her breath to contain her exuberant spirit. She can never shout out or open her window and greet the dawn. She is removed from the natural flow of the day and all the outside wonders and delights. Will this be the morning she and her family are discovered by the Nazis? How does she battle her fears and refuse to be ruled and oppressed by them? How does she remain an amazing life force and keep her humor in this, the worst of storms?

Morning Routines and Activities

Morning chores can help children to be cooperative and independent. These may be simple tasks like feeding the gerbils, watering the plants, gathering eggs, or making one's bed and cleaning one's room. More difficult tasks may involve children baking bread, shoveling snow, chopping and collecting wood, assisting a disabled parent, or helping take care of siblings.

The young farm girl in *Morning Milking* (Morris) loves her barn times with her father, washing the cows and putting on the milkers, and she is quite at home with the Holsteins and the Guernseys. It is obvious that she has the "touch," a natural ability to communicate with animals. For 9-year-old Eleanor in *My Prairie Year* (Harvey), each morning has a particular focus with "hard work" mornings extending into days—washing days, ironing days, mending days, and gardening days. But Sunday mornings after religious school are roaming days, wild and liberating, and well worth the wait.

Along with the chores, other activities can help give structure and continuity to the morning. There might be kitchen chats, story sharing, joke telling, and even wishing ceremonies. A parent and child might dress up a pet potato each morning to put in the child's lunchbox, easing that child's transition to school. Such rituals and routines serve to help begin the day in a fun, relaxed manner.

When routines are discarded, children can feel out of sorts. Their sense of order is threatened. If what they look forward to eludes them, they are likely to act out or pull inward. In *Breakfast with My Father* (Roy), David, whose parents are separated, eagerly anticipates his Saturday breakfasts with his father. On one

Saturday, when he thinks he is losing this sacred time, he is crushed, for this is something he counts on and something he needs.

The disruption of routines paralyzes Tommy in *Lazy Tommy Pumpkinhead* (DuBois), who lives in an electric house and is awakened, washed, powdered, dressed, and fed breakfast by a number of electric contraptions. What happens when the machines go haywire after a storm-induced power failure? This is a high-tech comic nightmare with a lesson about dependency. It presents the ultimate passive child, who ends up feeling like a "fat tomato in an omelet."

Morning Journeys

The journeys of the morning can lead children almost anywhere. In fact, any number of things, ordinary or astonishing, may engage them, even on the way to school. Such diversions may include sharing a joke with the doorman, scuffling on the school bus, stopping for a big, buttered bagel, picking ripe blueberries, spotting and catching a praying mantis, window shopping at the toy or hobby store, watching a movie being made, saying "hello" to the traffic guard, or playing "shimmy shimmy coco bop" with a friend before the second bell rings.

The fantasy-prone heroine in *The Trek* (Jonas) encounters jungle creatures, some docile and some dangerous, including a watermelon hippo and a forest of elephants. In her wild mind, lizards are crawling up the school building, and the school steps have become a treacherous mountain. No wonder she and her friend might enter class a little out of breath.

When Annamarie and Ellen in *Number the Stars* (Lowry) walk to school in German-occupied Denmark in 1943, they become cautious and less carefree when they pass pairs of leering soldiers on each street corner. They try to act natural, but the soldiers and their rifles have a strong, inhibiting presence.

In *Danny, the Champion of the World* (Dahl), a boy finds the morning walks with his father blissful and exhilarating. Through his father, a true naturalist, Danny learns about the marvels and habits of birds—their names, calls, and the ways they construct their nests. "Mostly it was he who talked and I who listened, and just about everything he said was fascinating."

Some children, in their journeys, head to places other than school. N'Tombi, in *N'Tombi's Song* (Seed), goes for the first time by herself to the trading store to buy sugar for her mother. Exuberant, barefoot, and 6 years old, N'Tombi enjoys being big and responsible and loves the feel and shininess of her silver coin. She thinks about the lovely purple flowers and juicy African plums and tries to bury her fears of the long-bearded snatching beast who may or may not be waiting in the forest.

Ahmed, in *The Day of Ahmed's Secret* (Heide), journeys with his donkey cart to an Egyptian marketplace to bring fuel to his customers. Along his route, there are all kinds of small pleasures—noodles and beans to eat, stories to share with the vendor Hassan, and daily stops at the thousand-year-old resting wall. There is much to stimulate and distract him—a constant swirl of colors, shapes, and sounds. But his thoughts stay focused on the secret he will share with his family, and he is feeling the deepest pride.

Creative Excursions

The Reveille Corner.   Younger children can create an exhibit of the ways people are awakened. They might display unusual types of alarm clocks and make a recording that would simulate rooster sounds, mockingbird calls, bugle songs, and train and factory whistles. They could also invent and design new "wake up" instruments or machines and invite others to enter a crowing contest.

Sweet and Sour Mornings.   After listening to *Alexander and the Horrible, No Good, Very Bad Day* (Viorst), younger children in small groups could illustrate, through short dramatizations, examples of both a sweet and sour morning. This session could begin with children discussing some of their own unforgettable mornings. A sweet morning might involve the birth of three rabbits, and a sour morning might involve the family dog eating up all the bacon.

The First Morning.   Younger or middle-grade children can listen to and discuss the African myth *The First Morning* (Bernstein and Kobrin), which explains how light came down from the sky to the earth through the cleverness of Mouse, Spider, and Fly. How was the Sky King outwitted, and what was inside the precious red box? Children could dramatize this myth or adapt it for a puppet show. They might want to use the same animal characters to create a play about what happens on the Second Morning.

On Being Late to School.   Younger or middle-grade children, after listening to *Late for School* (Reiss), could each try to concoct the most fantastic set of lies about why they are tardy, telling their story in a straight-faced and convincing manner. These lies could involve drastic weather changes or encounters with a babbling barracuda or a menacing platypus.

A Morning Collage.   Younger or middle-grade children, working in pairs, could each create a torn paper collage showing symbols of the morning and the wide range of morning activities. A collage might feature a toothbrush, a golden waffle, a giant dewdrop, or an unmade bed.

A Morning Promise.   Middle-grade children could each make a promise or resolution for the day, of something they would like to fulfill or strive for. These could be shared, written down, or kept in a journal.

. . . .

Hayley's Resolution

I resolve to follow more of my wishes. Sometimes I have ideas and dreams and I don't act on them. This makes me feel bad. I feel they get lost, and I am left with a desire to follow them.

Hayley Cuccinello, age 9

. . . .

Rooster in the Shade. Middle-grade children could dramatize a series of encounters involving a village rooster who, for some particular reason, has decided not to crow on this day. Now, in a thoughtful mood, the rooster sits in the shade of a willow tree waiting to see what might happen. Who in the village might be paying him a visit? Some possibilities:

- An unhappy child who missed seeing the sun come up.
- A worried farmer who was late milking his cow and feeding his pigs.
- An annoyed barber who did not have time to arrange his tonics or clean his clippers.
- An angry butcher who did not have time to cut and prepare his meats.
- An embarrassed judge who was late for court.

A Mysterious Morning. Middle-grade or older children, in the spirit of *The Twilight Zone* (Zicree), might create mysteries about someone who wakes up having changed or wakes up in a world different from their own. A baffled girl, for example, finds herself on the top bunk, but she does not even own a bunk bed. A strange silvery fish is swimming in her tank, and thick yellow moss is growing on the ceiling. What is more, the voice that calls the girl for breakfast is definitely not her mother's. This activity could be initiated by reading passages from *Rip Van Winkle* (Gipson) or showing scenes from the movie *Big* (Marshall).

A Morning Star Breakfast. Children of all ages could plan and make a special breakfast. They might prepare scones and milk from Ireland, bananas and peanut butter from Haiti, roasted corn from Peru, cornmeal mush and prairie hen gravy from *The Little House on the Prairie* (Wilder), pork sausage and biscuits from *Sounder* (Armstrong), or a *Johnny Appleseed* (Kellogg) breakfast that features apple juice, applesauce, baked apples, and apple turnovers. In a prebreakfast ceremony, someone might read aloud a poem—perhaps the African "Hymn to the Sun" from *Talking to the Sun* (Koch); "Brushing My Teeth" from *The Real Tin Flower* (Barnstone); or the underachiever's ode, "Today," from *Hey World, Here I Am!* (Little). A small group of singers could perform "Oh, What a Beautiful Morning" from *Oklahoma*; the Beatles song "Here Comes the Sun"; and the African American spiritual "My Lord, What a Morning."

Resources

Books

Ackerman, Karen. *By the Dawn's Early Light.* Atheneum, 1984.
Armstrong, William. *Sounder.* Harper and Row, 1969.
Banks, Lynne. *The Indian in the Cupboard.* Doubleday, 1985.
Barnstone, Aliki. "Brushing My Teeth," in *The Real Tin Flower.* Crowell, 1968.
Baylor, Byrd. *The Way to Start a Day.* Scribner, 1978.
Bernstein, Margery, and Kobrin, Janet. *The First Morning.* Scribner, 1976.
Carlstrom, Nancy. *Wishing at Dawn in Summer.* Little, 1993.

Carrick, Carol, and Carrick, David. *Sleep Out*. Clarion, 1973.

Dahl, Roald. *Danny, the Champion of the World*. Knopf, 1975.

Dorris, Michael. *Morning Girl*. Hyperion, 1992.

Dragonwagon, Crescent. *Katie in the Morning*. Harper, 1963.

DuBois, William. *Lazy Tommy Pumpkinhead*. Harper, 1986.

George, Jean. *My Side of the Mountain*. Dutton, 1965.

Gipson, Morrell. *Rip Van Winkle*. Doubleday, 1984.

Harvey, Brett. *My Prairie Year*. Holiday, 1986.

Heide, Florence. *The Day of Ahmed's Secret*. Lothrop, 1990.

Himler, Ronald. *Wake Up, Jeremiah*. Harper, 1979.

Holm, Anne. *North to Freedom*. Harcourt, 1965.

Hopkins, Lee Bennett. *Morning, Noon, and Nighttime, too*. Harper, 1980.

Jonas, Ann. *The Trek*. Greenwillow, 1985.

Kantrowitz, Mildred. *Willie Bear*. Four Winds, 1976.

Kellogg, Steven. *Johnny Appleseed*. Harper, 1988.

Koch, Kenneth. "Hymn to the Sun," in *Talking to the Sun*. Holt, 1985.

Kraus, Robert. *Milton the Early Riser*. Simon, 1972.

Lewis, Claudia. *Up in the Mountains*. Zolotow, 1991.

Little, Jean. "Today," in *Hey World, Here I Am!* Harper, 1986.

Lowry, Lois. *Number the Stars*. Houghton, 1989.

McCloskey, Robert. *One Morning in Maine*. Viking, 1952.

McPhail, David. *Farm Morning*. Harcourt, 1985.

Morris, Linda. *Morning Milking*. Picture Book, 1991.

Nolan, Dennis. *The Castle Builder*. Macmillan, 1987.

Peters, Lisa. *Good Morning, River!* Little, 1990.

Rattigan, Jama Kim. *Dumpling Soup*. Little, 1993.

Ray, Deborah. *Fog Drift Morning*. Harper, 1993.

Reiss, Mike. *Late for School*. Peachtree, 2003.

Roy, Ron. *Breakfast with My Father*. Houghton, 1980.

Sanders, Scott. *Aurora Means Dawn*. Bradbury, 1989.

Seed, Jenny. *N'Tombi's Song*. Beacon, 1987.

Shannon, George. "Three Rosebuds," in *Stories to Solve*. Greenwillow, 1985.

Shulevitz, Uri. *Dawn*. Farrar, 1974.

Shulevitz, Uri. *One Monday Morning*. Scribner, 1967.

Smalls, Irene. *Dawn and the Round-to-it*. Simon, 1994.

Smalls, Irene. *Irene and the Big, Fine Nickel*. Little, 1991.

Spinelli, Jerry. *Maniac Magee*. Little, 1990.

Uchida, Yoshiko. *Journey to Topaz*. Scribner, 1971.

Viorst, Judith. *Alexander and the Terrible, Horrible, No Good, Very Bad Day*. Atheneum, 1980.

Wahl, Jan. *Little Eight John*. Dutton, 1982.

Wilder, Laura Ingalls. *The Little House on the Prairie*. Harper, 1953.

Zicree, Marc. *The Twilight Zone Companion*. Silman, 1992.

Films, Videos, and DVDs

Big, directed by Penny Marshall. Fox, 1994. 104 minutes.

E.T., directed by Steven Spielberg. Universal, 1982. 115 minutes.

J.T. CBS Televison, 1969. 51 minutes.

The Twilight Zone-Collection 1, directed by Jos Addiss and William Asher. CBS, 1959. 25-minute episodes.

Sound Tracks

"Here Comes the Sun," from *Abbey Road,* written by George Harrison. Apple, 1969.

"My Lord What a Morning," from *Clarence Fountain and the Blind Boys of Alabama.* World Wide Gospel, 2000.

"Oh, What a Beautiful Morning," from *Oklahoma,* music by Richard Rodgers and lyrics by Oscar Hammerstein II. Capitol Records, 1947.

THEME 2:
Safe and Special Places ···●

Where am I welcome?

Where am I allowed to feel hopeful?

Where am I encouraged to create?

Where do I know the joys of banana pudding and bedtime stories?

Where will others take the time to listen to my jokes?

Where do I feel the most protected?

All children need to be in worlds where they feel free enough to express their emotions and dreams. In safe and healthy worlds, children know it is okay to flounder at times, to take a few tumbles, and to have a bad day. With encouragement and support, they learn to bounce back and be resilient.

So much of childhood is about exploring the first safe place of home and then branching out to find and create other safe places—a special corner, a reading rock, an indoor fort, or an outdoor castle.

It may be reassuring for children to describe some of the safe places they have known. Are these everyday places like home and school, or are they places in their memories and imaginations?

The range of children's perceived safe places is extremely diverse. For one child, a dress-up corner at school may be a safe place for experimenting with roles, re-creating family scenes, and trying out floppy hats, feathery boas, and all types of wild combinations.

For a hospitalized child, the pediatric playroom can be an oasis, a refuge, a safe place to escape from big medical terms and invasive needles. In this setting, a child can hook up with new friends who are facing similar struggles. They can break out for a time, share a good laugh, or engage in a freewheeling game of checkers.

For another child, the dance class or art studio can be a safe haven when the child's family is going through hard and volatile times. The rituals of a class can provide a comforting structure, and just working on a piece, whether personal or collaborative, can at times be exhilarating.

For a very young child, the children's room at the public library can be the safest place outside of home. Here, during story hour, a child can enjoy the delicious sounds of playful rhymes and the enchanting images of fairy-tale kingdoms. Here, a child will get to know a new and important adult, choose a special book to take home, and be welcomed into the story circle.

Each of the havens of childhood has its unique character and texture, and each has its specific set of images, sounds, and smells. When things get a bit tough and children are feeling insecure, they can retreat to their safe places, or at least conjure them up from their memories. In this way, they can once again experience feelings of solace and fellowship.

Children may find comfort in thinking about the signatures of home—the welcome mat or mezuzah, the African design on the bedroom wall, the blue crystal on the piano, the lilac scent of a favorite aunt's perfume, the hissing sound of a quirky radiator, or the lilting sound of a favorite lullaby. A child who loves sleepaway camp may pull out the sweet, stored images of wish boats floating on the camp lake under a robust moon. Another child, who feels especially safe at school, may be uplifted by the gentle sound of a rain stick like the one that calls her class together for meeting time.

A Literary Survey of Children's Safe Places

Often at the heart of children's books is the theme of having or needing a safe place in the world. What happens in these stories when a child journeys from home? What sustains that child? How do children deal with being homeless or displaced or living in a war-torn environment?

Being on mother's lap (Scott) provides Michael, a young Innuit boy, with feelings of coziness and infinite security. He loves the rocking rhythm of her chair and the softness of his reindeer blanket. There are also room for his doll and toy boat and even a little space for his puppy. The soothing picture book *Goodnight, Moon* (Brown) describes a child's bedroom, one of the first safe places of childhood. What a comforting and satisfying ritual it is for a child each night to survey his or her kingdom, contemplate each object, and take the time to say goodnight to "a comb and a brush and a bowl full of mush."

For Kevin and his Dad (Smalls), home is both a safe and joyful place where vacuuming rugs and folding laundry become delightful excursions. The two work hard, but their playful approach allows them to be inventive and lighthearted. Daniel in *Daniel's Duck* (Bulla) sees the hearth in his cabin as his safe place. Patiently carving a duck out of his block of wood, he is surrounded by his fiddle-playing father and quilt-making mother. Here, he can concentrate, basking in the warmth of the fire. He can join in conversations with others or think his own private thoughts about spring, the fair, and finishing his project. This close-knit family creates for Daniel a ring of protection.

In *A Salmon for Simon* (Waterton), the beckoning lights of Simon's cabin are among the important welcoming signs of home. As he runs toward the lights, he cannot wait to share his story about how he rescued a fish by creating a tunnel. He knows that his family loves and supports him and will be proud of his ingenuity.

As children grow more confident and secure, they may find safe places away from home—places out in the neighborhood and larger community. Some of these places help them to cultivate their aesthetic sides, lift their spirits, and stimulate their imaginations.

In *Ben's Trumpet* (Isadora), the title character likes to be near the smoky and seductive Zig Zag Club even though he is too young to go inside. It is the music that captivates him as it drifts out of the jazz club, permeating the street and inspiring him to want to make his own sounds and create his own riffs. Pamela, in *Pamela's First Musical* (Wasserstein), begins to tingle when she hears the overture of her first Broadway musical. She tingles again when she sees the exuberant dancers making their leaps and when an entire circus springs forth on the stage and then completely disappears. The playbill in Pamela's hand will become her link to this new and dazzling world—a world of elegance and magic.

For Matthew, in *The Car Washing Street* (Patrick), every Saturday reinforces his sense of being in a safe and special neighborhood as he watches the grown-ups outside soaping and polishing their cars. As the morning evolves, friendly splash fights occur. Someone begins to moonwalk; others form a conga line. A mood of playfulness prevails with neighbors joking and reminiscing while eating fruit-flavored ices on their stoops.

The barbershop in *Haircuts at Sleepy Sam's* (Strickland) and the beauty parlor in *Saturday at the New You* (Barber) are important fixtures in the neighborhood where children can find warmth and continuity, and everyone knows their names, even their preferred hair style. Works such as *It Takes a Village* (Cowen-Fletcher), *Harlem* (Myers), and *Just Plain Fancy* (Polacco) demonstrate the protective power of communities as well as the universality of this theme. In each of these places, children can wander about in a carefree way, knowing they are valued and cared for. They know that someone will reach out to them if they lose something, or if they stumble and hurt themselves.

Sometimes a safe place has to do with associations made with a special person and a series of shared adventures. In *The Raft* (LaMarche), *My Island Grandma* (Lasky), and *Grandaddy's Place* (Griffith), children are allowed to enter other worlds where they are nurtured and recognized and can express themselves fully.

Sometimes a safe place may involve other children and no grown-ups. The pretend town of Roxaboxen (McLerran), sitting high on a hill, is such a world. This charming town, built out of different-sized rocks and wooden boxes, has houses, shops, a town hall, a jail, and a one-grave cemetery, and children use pebbles as their currency. All of the children of Roxaboxen feel empowered by it, and quickly they learn to work things out and settle their differences.

For the introverted Ethan in *The View from Saturday* (Konigsburg), the place he feels the safest is at the weekly tea parties with his circle of friends who are known as the Souls. He is comfortable with his new pals who, like himself, enjoy books, puzzles, magic tricks, and intellectual challenges. Around them, he never has to apologize for being so smart, and, despite his shyness, he feels free enough to try out an original riddle.

On the opposite end of the spectrum are the four sixth graders in the film *Stand by Me*, who band together because they have been either abused or ignored. Their tree house is their one safe place, and only they know the secret knock. Once inside, they can bolster each other's spirits, and, despite their teasing and bantering, they acknowledge each other's gifts.

Sometimes safe places can become unsafe places. The young heroine in *A Chair for My Mother* (Williams) tries to remain hopeful after a devastating fire destroys her apartment. She sees that her mother is sad and wonders how she can help. Another child, Daniel in *Smoky Night* (Bunting), is forced to evacuate his home because of the Los Angeles riots. He worries about finding his cat Jasmine. He does not understand why there is so much rage around him and why people would destroy their own buildings.

Anne Frank, hiding with her family in an attic during World War II, knows that feeling safe happens for only tiny segments of time. Moments of pleasure can turn abruptly into moments of panic. A lovely dream or a quiet conversation with her friend Peter could be punctured by the sound of a siren or a loud knock on the door. Because of the undercurrents of fear and the claustrophobic living conditions, she can rarely relax or be at ease.

Wishing for a new home is what sustains the 9-year-old in *Junebug* (Mead). It helps him counter his feelings of resignation and defeat. Auburn Street Plaza, the project where he lives, can be a tense and spooky place. He is always waiting for the next fight to break out. He hates the stench in the stairway and the ugly words sprayed on the walls. Even his tenth-floor view is depressing. As he approaches the age of 10, he is trying to hatch a plan by using the bottles that he collects. On a family ferryboat ride, he will launch a fleet of fifty bottles—bottles with messages inside that will send his wish out into the world. This will be his ceremony of hope, his wild shot at turning his life around.

Dream Spots and Thinking Rocks

Where do children go when they need to be alone? Do they have any sort of retreat or sanctuary? Do they visit their climbing tree or thinking rock? Do they have a renewal place where they can take the time to meditate and ponder?

Some children, when feeling pinched and out-of-sorts, head off to their own, private thinking spot. Here, they can remove themselves from the intense dynamics of day-to-day family life and the resulting pressures and tensions. If they need to, they can sulk or rage or cry. They can replay in their minds a particular incident or work out a solution to a particular problem.

For others, having a special or secret place can make possible uninterrupted dreaming, drifting, and imagining. An ideal spot can be conducive to quiet, focused activity—perhaps sketching, reading, writing, composing, or acting out scenarios with plastic toy figures. With children overstimulated at times by a barrage of images and sounds, having a quiet place can help them cultivate their aloneness and become more independent and self-contained.

City children, in confined living spaces, may feel a strong need at times to distance themselves from others. For this reason, the title character in *Evan's Corner* (Hill) develops a space in the corner of his living room, making it his own with a plant, a painting, orange-crate furniture, and boundaries of rope. At last he has a retreat, a place to "sit alone and be content." This is his dreaming place where he can separate from family members and still have them close by. Having a corner will calm him when he is feeling stressed and enable him to feel centered and sane.

The dreamer in *Tar Beach* (Ringgold) finds solitude on her apartment roof, lying under the moon and stars, a short distance from her card-playing parents. Up here, she is safe and cool, and her mind can wander anywhere and travel at any speed. Up here, she can glide and soar through the luminous sky, claiming ownership of all things that attract her fancy.

Another urban dreamer conjures secret places (Brodsky) while painting, as she draws doorways that open into mysterious realms. She finds escape and tranquility as well through her piano playing. "In the secret place that is my music[,] I am far away. These are wordless hours when I live with my magic until suppertime."

Some children are lucky to have their special place outdoors in a meadow or lot, on a hill, or near a brook or quarry. A special place in the woods, for example, can yield many kinds of treats and treasures: the tastes of blueberries and honey; the smells of mint, lilac, and pine; even genuine arrowheads and artifacts from centuries past.

When children stay long enough in one place, they come to know its character, unique features, and amazing network of wildlife activity. Some may attach a name to an intriguing boulder or a dominating tree stump. An area thick with thorns and bristles might be called the Lizard's Nest. A steep, rocky area may be identified as Big Bear Ridge.

Certain dream spots can reconnect children to people who lived in times long ago. These haunted, spiritual grounds are often bountiful with clues. In the *Dreamplace* (Lyon), the Pueblo world of the Anasazi is like a "sandcastle built under a cliff." One might discover a prayer stick or grinding stone and feel the presence of the people "who built this dream, and who lit its wall with fire and stories." What happened here? Why did they disappear? And what secrets might the eagles know?

Another mystical place is described in *Where the Forest Meets the Sea* (Baker). An Australian boy and his father must take a boat to reach this primeval forest over 100 million years old. Once inside these woods, the boy imagines Aboriginal children playing among the twisted roots and hiding in secret tree hollows. What treasures did they own? What games did they play? How high could they climb? It seems that history is breathing here, and the boy feels the strangest, deepest connection. Observing intently, he sees their signs and hears their echoes.

A sculpture may haunt or inspire children with its powerful aura. In *The Green Lion of Zion Street* (Fields), neighborhood children miss their school bus because they are so caught up with the tantalizing stone lion. They dare each other to move in close to hold court with the "imperious" king. The fog helps sustain the illusion, adding that extra touch of mystery, and the children delight in being "half-scared." They squeal; they run; they speculate. Who is this stone cat anyway, and why does he cast such a spell?

The young boy who visits "the Wall" (Bunting) with his father is struck by the solemnity he feels and the little gifts that he sees (letters, flowers, flags, teddy bears). This Vietnam Veterans' Memorial, "black and shiny as a mirror," is an emotional setting, a place for ceremony and remembrance. The boy is awed and maybe overwhelmed by the endless list of names. How will they ever find the one that says," "George Munoz," which is the name of his grandfather?

A child may change his or her dream spot from time to time or keep it through all of childhood. Perhaps the best dream spots trigger in children rich and de-tailed fantasies.

The blind village boy, Hershel, in *Cakes and Miracles* (Goldin) finds his special place by the river where the water is soothing and liberating. The mud with its "cool smoothness" becomes his medium, allowing his hands to express what he sees in his dreams. The sounds and smells of the river help inspire his visions, and he is free to create tunnels, mountains, and all kinds of remarkable sculptures.

Having a private spot can help children shut out the pain when they are feeling fearful, disconnected, or misunderstood. These secret places can give them distance and breathing space and allow them to fantasize and reflect on things.

In the film *J.T.*, an emotionally wounded city boy finds a starving cat in an abandoned building. Something stirs in him, and he begins to feel playful and tender. He identifies with this friendless animal that is barely making it in the world, makes him an eye-patch and a makeshift stove house, and names him Mr. Bones. This decaying area becomes his hiding place. Here, he finds relief and does not have to think about his disappointed mother or worry about the two neighborhood bullies who are after his stolen radio.

The title character in *Petros' War* (Zei) is a 10-year-old Greek boy living in Athens during the German occupation. His imagination helps him to cope when the food is scarce and the mood is bleak. Only in his secret garden with his turtles and beetles does he feel protected. Here, he can relax, let down his guard, and dream and pretend. His fantasies of wearing armor and riding horses help to nourish him and preserve his spirit.

The medically challenged Freak in *Freak the Mighty* (Philbrick) does not have a particular spot. Instead, he retreats into the realm of books, especially works that chronicle the lives of King Arthur and Merlin. As a child who is tormented and teased and at risk in a number of ways, he is able to draw upon these legendary tales as a source of strength and inspiration. The ideals espoused in them help him to create his own personal code, and having a quest gives him a sense of purpose and direction. When he is immersed in his reading, the world becomes a brighter, safer, and more sensible place.

Creative Excursions

Imagining a Safe Place.   Uri Shulevitz's *Dawn* could inspire younger children to visualize a safe and peaceful place like the pond depicted in this story. Their imagined place could be on a mountain, by a waterfall, or in a clearing in the woods. They could then create a series of drawings and paintings so that they could share their safe places with others.

A Memory Place.   *When I Was Young in the Mountains* (Rylant) could lead younger children to interview some of the important adults in their life and have them recall the safe places in their childhood. Was their safe place in the kitchen where they made banana bread and pumpkin pudding from scratch? Was their safe place in the living room where the family made music together with fiddles and drums? Did they have a hideout in the attic or a secret place in the barn? How would they describe these places? Did they have different safe places at different ages?

About My Room.   Through discussion, younger and middle-grade children could reflect on their bedrooms. How is each child's room a sleeping place, a refuge, and a play area? How would children describe their room? Do they share it with anyone? Do they have a secret spot for their prized possessions? What kind of paper treasures do they keep on the walls—posters, photos, report cards, certificates? Where are the nightlights? What happens when children do not clean their rooms and are unable to camouflage all the mess and the dirt? Why do rooms get so cluttered, and why do parents and children so often go in rounds because of this issue? Some children might want to express their feelings about their room by writing a poem.

....

My Journey through My Dirty Room

I woke up and came out of my bed
and the covers were tangled on my legs.
I came out of the bed and stepped on a
hair clip.
Then my bike fell over and scratched
my leg.
I started screaming like crazy.
My hair looked crazy.
You could say I looked like
Frankenstein's wife.
Over the last few days my room
has really improved.
I mean the dirt is still there but the clips
and beads are gone.

Kaitlyn Cummings, age 9

....

The Right to a Safe Place. Middle-grade children could begin to define a safe place and then develop collectively, through writing and discussion, a decree, statement, or set of expectations.

"A safe place is where I am free of any bullies."

"A safe place is where people aren't always yelling."

"A safe place is where the grown-ups are paying attention and not just talking to each other."

"A safe place is where there are no toxins, poisons, or asbestos."

On My Thinking Rock. Middle-grade children can create monologues in which someone is sitting on a thinking rock, mulling things over or sorting things out. These can be first developed through writing and then dramatized. For example, a young girl goes to her thinking rock on the historical afternoon when Johnny Appleseed comes to visit her family. Outraged and annoyed, she cannot believe how much her family is carrying on, especially her mother.

Apple this, and apple that! I can't believe her—making apple fritters and apple pancakes and apple cider for the very same meal. And all that scrubbing and polishing—three dustings in one morning—and I'm the duster! And the way she's bossing everyone around—trying to put phony sugar-type words in our mouths, making us practice handshakes and curtsies. Well, I'm glad I broke that dish. I mean, why the big fuss? He's just a person, just a man with a bunch of seeds.

Designing a Meditation Room. Working individually or in pairs, middle-grade children could design a meditation room or contemplative environment. What materials would they need to actually build it? What would be its shape and texture? What colors would be emphasized? How would someone enter this space? Would there be chairs, pillows, or places for sitting? Would there be particular sounds and smells? Would there be a centerpiece—perhaps a mushroom sculpture, a rock garden, a mobile, or a miniature pool?

The Base Hog. Older children could develop a comic strip about a character that, during outdoor games, never leaves the base. This character might try to keep the base clean at all times, sweeping it, even decorating it. The base hog is very much at home here and not about to wander off, no matter what.

Olly, Olly in Free. Older children could investigate about the different kinds of bases, free squares, and safety zones that are found in both board games and outdoor games. Where or when is one safe in Freeze Tag, Stoop Tag, Kick the Can, and Capture the Flag? What board games have special protective devices like the "get out of jail free" cards in Monopoly? Some children may want to invent a game with all types of safety features.

A Universal Sculpture Garden. Older children can make clay or papier-mâché models of various sculptures from real life or literature. These might include the statues depicted in *Lentil* (McCloskey) and *Andy and the Lion* (Daugherty), the *Make Way for Ducklings* (McCloskey) statue in Boston Commons, the *Alice in Wonderland* (Carroll) sculpture in New York City's Central Park, *The Little Mermaid* (Andersen) in Denmark, *The Happy Prince* (Wilde) in Germany, the Thinker in France, the Sphinx in Egypt, or one of the giant stone figures on Easter Island. Some children might want to create sculptures to honor one of their favorite characters from mythology, folktales, or fiction.

Resources

Books

Andersen, Hans Christian. *The Little Mermaid.* Minedition, 2004.
Baker, Jeannie. *Where the Forest Meets the Sea.* Greenwillow, 1987.
Barber, Barbara. *Saturday at the New You.* Lee, 1994.
Brodsky, Beverly. *Secret Places.* Lippincott, 1979.

Brown, Margaret Wise. *Goodnight, Moon.* Harper, 1974.

Bulla, Clyde. *Daniel's Duck.* Harper, 1979.

Bunting, Eve. *Smoky Night.* Harcourt, 1994.

Bunting, Eve. *The Wall.* Clarion, 1990.

Cameron, Ann. *The Most Beautiful Place in the World.* Knopf, 1988.

Carroll, Lewis. *Alice's Adventures in Wonderland.* Holt, 1985.

Cowen-Flecher, Jane. *It Takes a Village.* Scholastic, 1994.

Daugherty, James. *Andy and the Lion.* Viking, 1938.

Fields, Julia. *The Green Lion of Zion Street.* McElderry, 1988.

Frank, Anne. *The Diary of a Young Girl.* Doubleday, 1967.

George, Jean. *My Side of the Mountain.* Dutton, 1959.

Goldin, Barbara. *Cakes and Miracles.* Viking, 1991.

Griffith, Helen. *Granddaddy's Place.* Greenwillow, 1987.

Hill, Elizabeth. *Evan's Corner.* Holt, 1967.

Himler, Ronald. *Wake up, Jeremiah.* Harper, 1979.

Holm, Ann. *North to Freedom.* Harcourt, 1965.

Holman, Felice. *Slake's Limbo.* Scribner, 1974.

Huck, Charlotte. *Secret Places.* Greenwillow, 1993.

Isadora, Rachel. *Ben's Trumpet.* Greenwillow, 1979.

Konigsburg, E. L. *The View from Saturday.* Atheneum, 1996.

Lakin, Patricia. *The Palace of Stars.* Tambourine, 1993.

LaMarche, Jim. *The Raft.* Harper, 2000.

Lasky, Kathryn. *My Island Grandma.* Warne, 1974.

Lomas Garza, Carmen. *Family Pictures.* Children's Book Press, 1990.

Lyon, George. *Dreamplace.* Orchard, 1993.

MacLachlan, Patricia. *All the Places to Love.* Harper, 1994.

McCloskey, Robert. *Lentil.* Viking, 1940.

McCloskey, Robert. *Make Way for Ducklings.* Viking, 1941.

McLerran, Alice. *Roxaboxen.* Lothrop, 1991.

Mead, Alice. *Junebug.* Farrar, 1995.

Mendoza, George. *And I Must Hurry for the Sea Is Coming In.* Prentice-Hall, 1969.

Myers, Walter Dean. *Harlem.* Scholastic, 1997.

Paterson, Katherine. *A Bridge to Terabithia.* Crowell, 1977.

Patrick, Denise. *The Car Washing Street.* Tambourine, 1993.

Philbrick, Rodman. *Freak the Mighty.* Scholastic, 1993.

Pinkwater, Daniel. *Wingman.* Dodd, 1975.

Polacco, Patricia. *Just Plain Fancy.* Bantam, 1990.

Rahaman, Vashanti. *Read for Me, Mama.* Boyds, 1977.

Ringgold, Faith. *Tar Beach.* Crown, 1991.

Rylant, Cynthia. *When I Was Young in the Mountains.* Dutton, 1982.

Scott, Ann. *On Mother's Lap.* McGraw, 1972.

Shulevitz, Uri. *Dawn.* Farrar, 1974.

Smalls, Irene. *Kevin and His Dad.* Little, 1999.

Spinelli, Jerry. *Maniac Magee.* Little, 1990.

Strickland, Michael. *Haircuts at Sleepy Sam's.* Boyds, 1998.

Wasserstein, Wendy. *Pamela's First Musical.* Hyperion, 1996.

Waterton, Betty. *A Salmon for Simon.* Atheneum, 1980.

Wilde, Oscar. *The Happy Prince and Other Tales*. Everyman, 1995.
Williams, Vera. *A Chair for My Mother*. Greenwillow, 1982.
Zei, Aliki. *Petros' War*. Dutton, 1972.

Films, Videos, and DVDs

Hope and Glory, directed by John Boorman. Columbia, 1987. 112 minutes.
J.T. CBS Television, 1969. 51 minutes.
Stand by Me, directed by Rob Reiner. Columbia, 1986. 87 minutes.

THEME 3:
Treasures .... ●

What makes something a treasure? What gives it special value? Where was it found, or how was it acquired? Which treasures are displayed on a child's dresser, and which ones are stored in secret places?

Some of these treasures might be special gifts from relatives and friends, souvenirs and mementos from family vacations, or old transitional objects like a tattered yarn doll, a lanyard made at summer camp, or a Mickey Mouse lunchbox with a broken handle.

But perhaps the most intriguing treasures are the ones discovered on hikes or in flea markets and junkyards. These treasures seem to stimulate all kinds of questions, and children like to speculate about their origins and journeys.

The title character in *Joe's Junk* (Russo) is an avid collector of treasures and scraps. Whenever he can, he meanders about—scouring alley and barn, closet and basement, always in search of gems forgotten.

In fact, Joe has a whole box of "S" things and boasts about owning the "world's largest indoor dump." His room is a repository of batteries, bolts, bicycle parts, shoelaces, and metal springs. Unfortunately, he has to deal with chagrined parents who are about to take drastic action because of all the clutter, chaos, and smells.

Paper Treasures

Why would a crumbling, yellow swim certificate prominently adorn a child's wall? Why would a fake diploma from a school fair be highlighted on a child's bedpost? What makes these paper treasures so important, and how might they be tied to other people?

If one were to navigate through the clutter of a child's bedroom, one might find a number of paper treasures that hint at the child's identity and character and illuminate his or her history. What documents are saved, and why?

Obviously, this is a selective process, a continual reassessing of what has worth and what can be discarded. Certain paper artifacts act as emotional keys for children, reopening the past and triggering a particular set of feelings. They allow children to hold on to pieces of time and to recall and savor the details of powerful experiences.

Paper treasures are both tangible and symbolic—touchstones that represent growth, prowess, coming of age. Some documents are enablers, permitting children to go on to the next step and entitling them to specific rights and privileges. There is something quite moving to see a child with his or her first library card, looking grown-up and proud, eager to feast on so many literary delights. All at once a child has access to a vast new story and information world and the power to journey, browse, and take books home.

Paper treasures often tell little success stories and reveal heartfelt triumphs. They serve to acknowledge talent, endurance, and achievement. They can stir

From *Theme Play: Exciting Young Imaginations* by Gary Zingher. Wesport, CT: Libraries Unlimited. Copyright © 2006.

romantic feelings and reconnect children to summertime friends and adventures. They can also ease the pain of uprooted children, helping them endure severe changes and stormy transitions. Just one photo or letter can rekindle hope and help combat the chaos and disruption.

Documents come in many forms and mean different things to different children. A bus pass may represent, to a child, freedom and mobility. An invitation might mean social acceptance. Other paper keepsakes include autographs, valentines, team pictures, class pictures, report cards, recipes, ticket stubs, and theater programs.

Scrapbooks and journals can be vehicles for helping children give shape and order to their lives. These highly personal documents encourage children to look inward, be reflective, and cultivate their pensive sides. Putting together a scrapbook can be an exciting and creative venture as children figure out ways to catalog events and animate each section. Keeping a journal allows children to record their journeys. Here, they are free to ponder and probe, dream and conjecture, and through their entries, they can attain closure, move on, and separate from each day.

Many books could spark younger children's interest in this theme and encourage them to bring in their own paper treasures and those saved by parents and grandparents. Books such as *A Letter to Amy* (Keats) and *Secret Valentine* (Stock) show the care and concern that can be invested by children in reaching out to others, both special friends and strangers. As illustrated in *Stringbean's Trip to the Shining Sea* (Williams), postcards can help children recall the highlights (and low points) of a summer's odyssey—everything from circus trains on the road to purple mountains at sunset.

Family recipes are at the heart of *The Miracle of the Potato Latkes* (Penn) and *The High Rise Glorious Skittle Skat Roarious Sky Pie Angel Food Cake* (Willard). In the first story, Tante Golda's golden latkes are reflections of her generosity and sense of community, her willingness to share even her "last tiny potato with a beggar." In the second story, a young girl begins to value her great-grandmother's legacy as she searches through thirty-two notebooks to find a particular recipe.

Ideas for creating a scrapbook and arranging the contents are lovingly rendered in *Carl Makes a Scrapbook* (Day) and *Li'l Sis and Uncle Willie* (Everett). The Uncle Willie referred to in the second title is William H. Johnson, the acclaimed African American painter.

The Trading Game (Slote) should appeal to any child who has ever been obsessed with baseball cards. Why is the book's hero, Andy Harris, determined to obtain the Ace 459 baseball card even though it has so little market value? How does this card tie him to his deceased father? What does he learn about wheeling and dealing and playing fair, and how does he resolve his conflict with his grandfather?

In *Dear Mr. Henshaw* (Cleary), a lonely, disconnected Leigh Botts is able to deal with some of the absurdities of home and school through an exchange of letters with his favorite author. Leigh's own letters prove to be satirical and wise and help him acquire perspective in an often cockeyed world.

Older children should find the historical novel *A Gathering of Days* (Blos) a thoughtful and vivid account of New England life in the early 1830s. Catherine Cabot Hill, age 13, chronicles in her journal everything from the gentle praise she receives from her father to the fury and impact of a harsh New Hampshire winter. Ultimately, the journal comes to serve as her internal sounding board. It helps her come to terms with the illness and death of her best friend, Cassie, and the moral dilemma of Teacher Holt, who sought to expand the curriculum, guiding students to grapple with the issue of slavery.

A Handful of Stars (Schami) also has a strong sense of detail, portraying the day-to-day human dynamics in a poor section of Damascus in the 1960s. The hero's journal is his secret outlet for raising questions and expressing dissent in a highly repressive society.

Some children may become collectors of words. Donavan, the title character in *Donavan's Word Jar* (DeGross), is a passionate collector. He writes down words that spark his interest on little slips of yellow paper and keeps them in a glass jar.

Always observant, he collects words from everywhere—from cereal boxes, shop signs, billboards, even parades. But he snatches most of his words from people's conversations.

From his word jar, whenever he wishes, he can pull out a word like "lullaby" that will calm him, or words like "extraterrestrial" or "zeppelin" that arouse his sense of adventure. Owning words like "hieroglyphic" and "serendipity" makes him feel intelligent, and a word like "emporium," which he got from his grandma, gives him a sense of history and of changing times.

With his vocabulary constantly expanding and his jar getting fuller, Donavan must figure what to do with so many words. He has a problem to solve and seeks the advice of important grown-ups. Should he find a different type of container, or should he alphabetize his words and put them in a book?

At last he finds his solution at his grandma's, when he visits her lounge and introduces his words to her bickering neighbors. He sees how these words tickle them, encouraging their interplay and somehow changing their mood. All of a sudden there are harmony and laughter, and everyone seems engaged, from the "persnickety" Miz Mary Lou to the "cantankerous" Bill Gut.

Feeling generous, he decides to no longer hoard his words. Instead, from time to time, he will simply give them away.

Pocket Rocks

What are the treasures that children may carry with them on their everyday journeys? How many of them own a pocket rock, and how might owning such a rock make them feel safe and omnipotent?

Byrd Baylor, the author of *Everybody Needs a Rock*, is passionate and philosophical about the subject of rocks, especially the small-sized rocks that become personal treasures. She knows their importance in childhood and offers guidelines for finding and selecting them. Choosing a rock, she explains, is a very private and thoughtful process—one that requires checking out each potential rock from different angles and perspectives. How does it feel in a child's palm? How does it fit in a child's pocket?

Among the qualities to consider, she points out, are the size and shape of the rock, the color, the flatness and smoothness, and even the smell (which can reveal clues about the rock's origin and history). "Some kids can tell by sniffing whether a rock came from the middle of the earth or from an ocean or from a mountain where wind and sun touched it every day for a million years."

Just one pocket rock can stimulate a child's imagination and sense of wonderment. It can connect a child to the natural world, to time and history. What are the secrets of a newly found stone? Could it have been used by a stuttering boy named Demosthenes? Could it have once been part of a Native American campsite, a stone wall in New England, or a famous General's tomb? Is it a rock that could make a child feel secure because it seems to have protective powers? Could it be a wishing rock or a rock to be used for starting a fire? Does it have the size and weight to be a good hopscotch rock? How might it look in a garden? How might it skim on water?

There are a number of celebrated rocks in children's books. Think of the pebbles used by the clever crow to obtain water from the bottom of a pitcher. Think of the stones that become important cooking ingredients in the tale of *Stone Soup* (Brown). Think of the rocks used by the children of Roxaboxen (McLerran) as pretend money for roleplaying games.

Sometimes there are distinctive rocks with unusual markings that may be imbued with magical or special qualities. These are rocks that journey through time and may become touchstones in the lives of their keepers. Where do these rocks come from, and what stories would they have to tell?

The pebble in *Sylvester and the Magic Pebble* (Steig) is "flaming red" and "perfectly round like a marble." A donkey named Sylvester finds the pebble and is astonished to find out that it can grant his wishes. Now he can make the rain go away, and, when he chooses, he can make it come back. With a generous heart, he is eager to share his gift with family and friends.

The stone in *The Lucky Stone* (Clifton) is "shiny and black as night." A runaway slave girl named Mandy scratches an "A" on it and uses it in a mysterious way to let people know that she is hiding in a cave so that they will bring her some food. The same stone is passed down, years later, to her daughter Vashti, who keeps it in a pouch around her neck. One day, in church, she is saved from death when her stone falls off and she goes to retrieve it. At that very second, a bolt of lightning strikes the exact spot where she was just standing.

The rock in *The Worry Stone* (Dengler) is an irregular, brown stone "with little hills and valleys on its surfaces." It belongs to a girl named Amanda who lives in California's Ojai Valley. This stone helps to ease her sorrow when her grandfather dies, absorbing some of her pain. He was the one who explained its origin, why it feels wet and smooth, and how it is tied to a young man's tears.

Lucky Pennies

Heads!
Tails!
Heads!
Tails!

Flip a penny.
Toss a penny.

Spin a penny.
Win a penny.

Find a penny.
Lose a penny.

A penny for your thoughts.
A penny for a magic trick.
A penny for a loafer.
A penny for a cinnamon stick.

What can happen to a penny?
And where will its journey end?

In a wishing pond?
On a railroad track?

In a blue jay's nest,
Or a sidewalk crack?

In the President's pocket,
Or a peddler's sack?

Where will its journey end?

To discover a rare and shiny penny in an obscure or hidden place is one of the delights of childhood, and pennies can end up anywhere, sometimes remaining hidden for years.

Children love pennies. They love the hardness, shininess, and the way they make a "plink" when dropped inside a big glass jar. They love looking at the date on a penny to see if it matches the date of their birth. They like to count pennies, collect them, roll them, and put them in piggy banks and gumball machines.

Children like to make piles of pennies, stacking them in tens and twenties. How high can they make their penny tower before it comes crashing down? They use pennies in crackling street games and simple magic tricks. Some children can make a penny disappear; others can make a penny spin. Many use them in their wishing rituals, tossing them with an abundance of hope into a pond, a well, or a fountain.

An African American boy named Michael, in *The Hundred-Penny Box* (Mathis), loves emptying, then counting, the pennies from his Great-Great-Aunt Dew's "cracked-up, wacky-dacky" wooden box. Every penny in the hundred-penny box carries a story or two, a memory, a nugget of history.

Simply hearing the date of a particular coin can trigger Aunt Dew's powerful sense of recall, and she is able to summon up all kinds of events, details, and feelings. Through this ritual of looking at pennies, Michael learns about the Reconstruction and the Depression.

If there were such a thing as "penny language," then Michael and Aunt Dew would be experts in the field. Examining and reading pennies are the way they connect and come together, and the activity itself is an expression of their intimacy.

When Michael's mother wants to get rid of the dilapidated penny box, he feels compelled to take charge and prevent this from happening. He knows that this container is both a treasure box and a time capsule. Captured in each coin are the stories of a survivor, and the coins, in sequence, provide the chronology of an extraordinary life.

In *Penny on the Road* (Precek), a Pennsylvania boy in 1973, on his way to school, reaches into a puddle when he spies something "flat and round and dark." What he retrieves, to his amazement, is a 1793 penny. This small treasure sets his imagination flying. He begins to wonder about its history, how it got there, and about the kinds of vehicles that used this very road, "maybe even a covered wagon."

He tries to conjure in his mind the image of a boy who might have lost the penny. Would he be wearing shoes? Would he be plowing the fields? Would he be taking time off to hunt for worms so that later he could go fishing?

Even in school, he cannot stop thinking about this boy. Did he get along with the schoolmaster? How did he spend his recess time? Was he good at marbles? Was he the kind of boy who won every race? What would they share in common? Would they laugh at the same kind of jokes?

The boy knows that this is a penny to save—a rare and glistening penny that deserves its own special pouch. It is a penny that arouses his emotions and connects him to another time. It is clearly a powerful penny, one that would always transport him and tickle his curiosity.

There are a number of terrific penny stories. Alvin Schwartz, in *Whoppers*, describes a man so cheap that he paid his children a penny each for not eating their dinner. At night, while they were sleeping, he would steal the pennies back. In the film *Stand by Me*, the worrywart, Vern, spends hours under his house digging holes to find the spot where he had buried his penny jar. The more he digs, the more his jar eludes him. If only he had made a secret sign or marker. Instead, he has created a prairie dog's paradise.

Box and Bin, Trunk and Tin

What are the kinds of containers that might be used for storing treasures? What are their sizes and shapes, and from what materials are they made?

In *A Pocket for Corduroy* (Freeman), a toy bear's quest to make a pocket for himself during a trip to the Laundromat ends up being a scary, soapy, lonely episode. When his owner Lisa finds him at last and then makes him a pocket, sewing it on his overalls, Corduroy is delighted and relieved. He especially likes that she puts a card inside with his name on it.

Eeyore, the donkey in *Winnie the Pooh* (Milne), loves his "very useful pot"—a birthday present from his friend Pooh. He loves it, surprisingly, for the simplest reason. He can put something in it and then take it back out. Repeating this over and over gives him sublime satisfaction.

Corduroy's pocket and Eeyore's useful pot are just two of the classic containers in children's stories. Others include the Houdini box (Selznick), the hundred-penny box (Mathis), Anno's mysterious multiplying jar, the flying trunk (Lewis), the Zimwi's drum (Aardema), Little Fox's deerskin pouch (Keeler), Gregory's chalk box (Bulla), and Wilfred Gordon McDonald Partridge's shoe box of treasures (Fox). These containers are integral to their stories and may serve as vessels, carriers, or storage places. In *The Secret of the Matchbox* (Willis), the secret turns out to be a tiny dragon. In *The Invasion* (Applegate), a plain blue box endows those who touch it with a remarkable power.

Certain containers are symbolic to children. They can represent, in concrete terms, different stages of development. Katie, the little sister in *The Purse* (Caple), has mixed feelings about her new and shiny yellow plastic purse. She faces the dilemma of what to put in it and later is not pleased with the sound that it makes whenever she shakes it. Sacrificing her Band-Aid box was the practical, grown-up thing to do, but now she misses the wonderful clinking noise that the metal box could produce when she marched around jingling her coins.

The younger brother in *I Need a Lunch Box* (Caines) obsesses about owning a lunch box as his school-age sister prepares to enter first grade. He fantasizes about what color it might be and how it might be designed. He is not interested, though, in storing food. He wants a lunch box so he can carry around his crayons and marbles.

Some containers can help link children to distant places as they cope with feelings of separation and loss. When Louie in *The Trip* (Keats) moves to an apartment in a new neighborhood, he re-creates his old turf in a shoe box by using crayons, paper, and glue. When he completes his project, he can peek inside the hole in the box and wander in his mind around his old street where all the details are vivid and familiar. He can encounter old friends and experience the sweetness and security that come from being recognized and accepted.

Similarly, Jamie Ramos, in *The Magic Shell* (Mohr), who moved to New York City from the Dominican Republic, has a special container that can help him deal with his homesickness. His container, given to him by his great-uncle Ernesto, is a conch shell. By holding the magic shell to his ear, he can conjure up the images, sounds, and scents of the balmy island for which he aches. The wise Ernesto had explained, "You must be quiet and concentrate and listen carefully. You will hear the roaring sea and soon you will have memories of home—of our mountain village where the skies touch heaven and the earth smiles down at the sea."

Other containers are tied to giving and sharing. These containers and their contents spark the imagination, stimulate playmaking, and can bring together individuals of different ages and generations. The eccentric Joseph in *All the Magic in the World* (Hartmann) invites neighborhood children to play with the treasures in his tin and to learn the secrets of making string art and turning soda can rings into silver chains.

The grandmother in *The Button Box* (Reid) introduces her grandchild to an entire button universe—buttons with and without holes, buttons made out of velvet, metal, wood, antlers, and seashells. These buttons demand careful inspection, for each has its own character. These are also buttons that have stories to tell—stories about fancy parties, military parades, and royal intrigues.

In *The Song and Dance Man* (Ackerman), when the retired vaudevillian opens his "dusty brown, leather-trimmed trunk," the attic permeates with the "smell of cedar chips and old things saved." In minutes, he is able to transport his grandchildren to another era and treat them to a live performance of jokes, tricks, dances, and songs. With his bowler hat, vest, and "half-moon silver taps," he enthralls and delights them by sharing both his talent and legacy.

Almost all children have special containers that they keep somewhere in their rooms. These might include a glass jar for catching fireflies, a locket with a photo of a friend, a beach pail, a snow shaker, a cricket cage, a dinosaur bank, or a valentine-shaped candy box filled with letters and pieces of lace. Children could describe one of their containers in terms of its size, shape, color, marking, weight, texture, age, and durability. What do they keep inside—baseball cards, photos, bottle caps, or charms? How did they come by it? Was it bought, found, or made at school or camp? Did a family member, friend, or stranger give it to them? On a special sharing day, children could each bring in a container for others to examine and enjoy.

Creative Excursions

Rock Games. Younger children could invent games using rocks of different shapes and sizes. They could hold a hopscotch tournament or teach each other how to play "Mancala" or "Rock, Paper, Scissors."

A Wall of Good Feelings. Younger or middle-grade children could each bring in a paper treasure or souvenir—one that evokes warm memories. These mementos can be shared with the group and then exhibited on a wall. These might include certificates of achievement, community service badges, stamps from abroad, menus, maps, letters from pen pals, photos from family outings, origami figures, and original cartoons.

Folk Character Bookmarks. Middle-grade children could create bookmarks in the shape of their favorite folk character—perhaps Tattercoats (Jacobs), John Henry (Keats), or one of the Three Strong Women (Stamm). Some children might want to make their bookmark in the shape of a famous literary prop such as the Zimwi's drum (Aardema) or Bony-Leg's bathtub (Cole).

The Junk Market. This is a storytelling activity. Middle-grade children could pretend to be objects at a junk market that come to life and share their tales and histories. These might include a hat rack that once lived in the White House and served three different presidents, a tattered umbrella that reminisces about how it survived one of the great rainstorms of the century, and a Persian lamp that shares enchanting tales about a singing beggar, an evil-eyed wizard, and a princess who smells like jasmine.

What Is a Penny Worth? Middle-grade children could carefully examine what is on a penny and find information about how pennies are minted. They might want to learn about Eagle Head pennies and find out why 1943 pennies are made of steel rather than copper. They could interview grandparents to find out what a penny could buy when they were children. They could also try to find out why so many people leave pennies on Benjamin Franklin's grave.

A Penny Fair. Middle-grade children could develop a penny fair. Visitors could try the penny toss and other games at the penny arcade; build a penny tower; estimate the number of pennies in a jar; buy homemade penny candy; browse through an exhibit of unusual piggy banks; watch a puppet show about Henny Penny—the panicky hen; pick a paper flower from the Pennyworth Garden; audition for the Ten Penny Players; make up a penny riddle ("Why did the penny cross the road?"); or take a leisure stroll down Penny Lane, listening to the tunes of a pennywhistle band.

The Box and Tin Museum. Middle-grade children could create a museum featuring a Chinese riddle box, a music box, a jack-in-the-box, a bottle with a ship inside, a Russian matryoshka doll, and such classic story containers as Fagin's treasure box, Blanche's basket of talking eggs (San Souci), Ada Potato's violin case (Caseley), Donovan's word jar (DeGross), and the Sky God Nyame's golden box of stories (Haley). As museum guides, children could explain the importance of each container and read passages from those stories cited.

> So Ananse took the golden box of stories back to earth, to the people of his village. When he opened the box, all the stories scattered to the corners of the world, including this one. (*A Story, A Story*, Haley)

A Lucky Object Museum. Middle-grade children could create a lucky object museum where they exhibit their charms, lockets, rings, ring stones, wishbones, horseshoes, dream catchers, and the lucky pieces of their parents and grandparents. In a special exhibit, they could display famous lucky objects from stories—the amazing bone (Steig), the magic fan (Baker), and the feather from *Birdsong* (Haley). They might also want to have a museum gift shop that features handmade good-luck pouches and miniature fountains.

Literary Logs. Middle-grade children as literary characters could write three or four journal entries that reveal their character's passions, secrets, and concerns. What were the private thoughts and yearnings of Queenie Peavy (Burch)? What were Homer Price's reactions to the donut fiasco (McCloskey)? Why did Junior Brown (Hamilton) feel alienated, and how did he perceive others in his world? What touched and surprised Jo March when she browsed through the treasures of her sister Beth (Alcott)? What were Miyax's first impressions of the Arctic wolf pack that became such a vital part of her existence (George)?

The Box People. Middle-grade children could each become a box character by creating a costume out of cardboard and then inviting others to come and meet them and learn about their special abilities. Among the Box People might be Mr. Juke Box, who will play any tune on his musical menu, the Toolbox Kid, who can repair almost anything with her variety of tools, and Shadowbox Sue, who can create magical images with her puppets and lights.

Treasure Box Plays. Middle-grade and older children could develop miniature dramas inspired by a treasure chosen from a treasure box. These treasures might include a stone, a stick, and a gourd.
Some possible "stone" scenarios:

- A special stone is used in the world champion hopscotch game.
- A stone is used by a clever crow to get water from out of a pitcher.
- Three fools argue over the best way to make stone soup.
- Someone is skimming a stone on the water when an angry mermaid pops up.

Some possible "stick" scenarios:

- A frazzled sorceress misplaces her magic wand.
- A magician tries to keep peace between his violin and bow.
- In the Cheap Olympics, the same stick is used as a chinning bar, racing baton, javelin, and pole-vaulting pole.
- Two conniving giants plot to steal the maypole from the forest elves so they can use it as a toothpick.

Some possible "gourd" scenarios:

- A gourd brings good luck to a family at harvest time.
- A meteor lands on the Earth from the Planet of the Gourds.
- An inept fairy godmother tries to transform a gourd into a coach.
- A secret ceremony involves the hatching of the purple-crested "guordo" bird.
- Someone is selling gourdware from door to door.

Pretend Scrapbooks. Middle-grade or older children, working individually or in pairs, could invent a person with a special talent and create a scrapbook based on that person's life. On the cover can be a drawing, silhouette, or caricature of the person. Devised documents inside might include a birth certificate, baby picture, spelling test, winning raffle ticket, high school diploma, wedding invitation, fake newspaper clipping, passport, telegram, and a "thank you" note. A strong personality should emerge from simply scanning the pages. An example of a fictitious character might be Whiz McKee, the best whistler in Wackanack County who once whistled for the President in the White House, or Felice Fremont, who combined her love of music and mammals to compose the Armadillo's Opera. This project was originally suggested in *At the Pirate Academy: Adventures with Language in Library Media Center* (Zingher).

The Mysterious Stone. Middle-grade or older children, through creative writing, could develop the third Harris Burdick mystery (Van Allsburg) into a story. Why does the third stone keep coming back when the boy skims it in the water? Does the stone have a power of its own? Is it carried back by a magical wave? Is it a dolphin, mermaid, or water sprite that sends the stone back in order to make contact with the boy? Some children instead may want to create original tales about an iridescent stone, a stone that hums, a stone with a message on it, or a cursed stone from a great pyramid.

Literary Trunks. Middle-grade or older children could create activity trunks for younger children, each based on a specific book. A *Charlotte's Web* (White) trunk might contain a tape of barnyard sounds, a design-a-web kit, a county fair ribbon-maker, a "fantastic" word game, and a Templeton the Rat poster. A *Jack and the Beanstalk* (Kellogg) trunk might include a beanbag toss game, a magic bean cookbook, beanstalk climbing instructions, a thumb harp, a golden egg-dyeing kit, and a sound recording of the grumbling giant. A *Treasure Island* (Stevenson) trunk might offer pirate language flashcards, a pirate hat-making kit, a parrot puppet project, a treasure map, a miniature mop and bucket for swabbing the deck, and a Long John Silver board game.

The Commissioner of Rocks. Older children could develop an improvised play about the Commissioner of Rocks, who surveys his or her world each day to make sure there are no problems, no infractions, no breaking of the rules. What happens when the Commissioner encounters:

• A pebble polisher who is working much too slowly.
• A rock star who is wearing too many rhinestones.
• A soup chef who is scrimping on stones while making stone soup.
• A daring child who is sitting on a recreational rock without having a permit.

Resources

Books

Aardema, Verna. *Bimwili and the Zimwi.* Dial, 1985.
Ackerman, Karen. *The Song and Dance Man.* Knopf, 1988.
Alcott, Louisa. *Little Women.* Grosset, 1983.
Anno, Mitsumasa. *Anno's Mysterious Multiplying Jar.* Putnam, 1983.
Applegate, K. A. *The Invasion.* Scholastic, 1996.
Baker, Keith. *The Magic Fan.* Harcourt, 1989.
Baylor, Byrd. *Everybody Needs a Rock.* Aladdin, 1974.
Blos, Joan. *A Gathering of Days.* Scribner, 1979.
Brown, Marcia. *Stone Soup.* Atheneum, 1947.
Bulla, Clyde. *The Chalk Box Kid.* Random, 1987.
Burch, Robert. *Queenie Peavy.* Viking, 1966.
Caines, Jeannette. *I Need a Lunch Box.* Harper, 1988.

Caple, Kathy. *The Purse*. Houghton, 1986.
Caseley, Judith. *Ada Potato*. Greenwillow, 1989.
Caudill, Rebecca. *A Pocketful of Cricket*. Holt, 1964.
Cleary, Beverly. *Dear Mr. Henshaw*. Morrow, 1983.
Clifton, Lucille. *The Lucky Stone*. Delacorte, 1979.
Coerr, Eleanor. *Sadako and the Thousand Paper Cranes*. Putnam, 1977.
Cole, Joanna. *Bony-Legs*. Scholastic, 1986.
Day, Alexandra. *Carl Makes a Scrapbook*. Farrar, 1994.
DeGross, Monalisa. *Donavan's Word Jar*. HarperCollins, 1994.
Dengler, Marianna. *The Worry Stone*. Rising Moon, 1996.
Everett, Gwen. *Li'l Sis and Uncle Willie*. Hyperion, 1994.
Fitzhugh, Louise. *Harriet the Spy*. Harper, 1964.
Fox, Mem. *Wilfred Gordon McDonald Partridge*. Kane, 1985.
Freeman, Don. *A Pocket for Corduroy*. Viking, 1978.
Gans, Roma. *Rock Collecting*. Harper, 1984.
Garfield, Brian. *Hopscotch*. Lippincott, 1975.
George, Jean. *Julie of the Wolves*. Harper, 1972.
Greenblatt, Rodney. *Aunt Ippy's Museum of Junk*. Harper, 1991.
Haley, Gail E. *Birdsong*. Knopf, 1988.
Haley, Gail E. *A Story, A Story*. Atheneum, 1970.
Hamilton, Virginia. *The Planet of Junior Brown*. Simon, 1971.
Hartmann, Wendy. *All the Magic in the World*. Dutton, 1973.
Hurt, Carol Otis. *Rocks in His Head*. Greenwillow, 2001.
Jacobs, Joseph. *Tattercoats*. Putnam, 1989.
Keats, Ezra Jack. *John Henry*. Knopf, 1987.
Keats, Ezra Jack. *A Letter to Amy*. Harper, 1968.
Keats, Ezra Jack. *The Trip*. Mulberry, 1978.
Keeler, Katharine. *Little Fox*. Macmillan, 1932.
Kellogg, Steven. *Jack and the Beanstalk*. Harper, 1991.
Lewis, Naomi. *The Flying Trunk and Other Stories from Hans Andersen*. Prentice, 1986.
Madian, Jan. *Beautiful Junk*. Little, 1968.
Mathis, Sharon Bell. *The Hundred-Penny Box*. Puffin, 1986.
McCloskey, Robert. *Homer Price*. Viking, 1943.
McLerran, Alice. *Roxaboxen*. Lothrop, 1991.
Medearis, Angela. *Picking Peas for a Penny*. Scholastic, 1990.
Milne, A. A. *Winnie the Pooh*. Dutton, 1954.
Mohr, Nicholosa. *The Magic Shell*. Scholastic, 1995.
Penn, Malka. *The Miracle of the Potato Latkes*. Holiday, 1994.
Pfister, Marcus. *Milo and the Magical Stones*. North, 1997.
Precek, Katharine. *Penny on the Road*. Macmillan, 1989.
Reid, Margarette. *The Button Box*. Dutton, 1990.
Russo, Susan. *Joe's Junk*. Holt, 1982.
San Souci, Robert. *The Talking Eggs*. Dial, 1980.
Schami, Rafik. *A Handful of Stars*. Dutton, 1990.
Schwartz, Alvin. *Whoppers, Tall Tales and Other Lies*. Harper, 1975.
Selznick, Brian. *The Houdini Box*. Knopf, 1991.
Slote, Alfred. *The Trading Game*. Lippincott, 1990.

Small, David. *Paper John*. Farrar, 1987.

Stamm, Claus. *Three Strong Women: A Tall Tale from Japan*. Viking, 1990.

Steig, William. *The Amazing Bone*. Farrar, 1976.

Steig, William. *Sylvester and the Magic Pebble*. Windmill, 1969.

Stevenson, Robert Louis. *Treasure Island*. Gramercy, 2002.

Stewig, John. *Stone Soup*. Holiday, 1991.

Stock, Catherine. *Secret Valentine*. Bradbury, 1991.

Tagore, Rabindranath. *Paper Boats*. Caroline, 1992.

Van Allsburg, Chris. *The Mysteries of Harris Burdick*. Houghton, 1984.

White, E. B. *Charlotte's Web*. Harper, 1952.

Willard, Nancy. *The High Rise Glorious Skittle Skat Roarious Sky Pie Angel Food Cake*. Harcourt, 1990.

Williams, Karen Lynn. *Galimoto*. Lothrop, 1990.

Williams, Vera. *A Chair for My Mother*. Greenwillow, 1982.

Williams, Vera. *Springbean's Trip to the Shining Sea*. Greenwillow, 1988.

Williams, Vera. *Three Days in a River in a Red Canoe*. Greenwillow, 1981.

Willis, Val. *The Secret in the Matchbox*. Farrar, 1988.

Wyler, Rose. *Secrets in Stone*. Four Winds, 1970.

Zingher, Gary. *At the Pirate Academy: Adventures with Language in the Library Media Center*. ALA, 1990.

Films, Videos, and DVDs

Stand by Me, directed by Rob Reiner. Columbia, 1986. 89 minutes.

THEME 4:
Imagining and Pretending··●

I am on the make-believe team.
I can act! I can dream!

I can be whatever I wish.
A clumsy fox. An elegant fish.

I am a downbird without my wings,
Or any one of a thousand kings.

I am a star in the licorice sky.
I am the June bug that stayed for July.

Those young people often identified as dreamers may need time every day to create and experiment. Such children are usually self-contained and self-propelled, thoughtful explorers of the worlds they inhabit. To them, any image or sound can be a starting point for a possible excursion. They look at things with a special sensitivity, always seeing the drama, the humor, the poetry. They like to make up story lines, invent characters and costumes, and play with words and ideas.

The heroine in *Amazing Grace* (Hoffman), for example, is rarely bored because she is a pretender and an adventuress. She is collecting stories all the time, and they become the content of her imaginative journeys as she brings each of the stories to life.

Grace is her own one-girl rep company, leaping from character to character, from Anansi to Joan of Arc, from Mowgli to Aladdin. Sometimes others will join in her pretend play, and they include her cat, her Ma, and her Nana.

But often she pretends alone, joyfully acting out her beloved scenarios. Agile and resourceful, Grace knows that she can be anyone or anything, traveling to all times and places. Her imagination is her passport, and her Ma and Nana are her nurturers.

Drac and the Gremlin (Baillie) takes a peek at two pretenders who join forces to develop an elaborate fantasy. They, too, love to dress in costumes and to become specific characters with strong personalities.

They especially like to be heroic and to go on quests, and their playmaking involves such elements as the capture, the rescue, and the escape. Naturally, there are obstacles to overcome and many scary and suspenseful moments.

These two incorporate whatever they see into their play, inventing their story and creating their dialogue as they go along. The top of a garbage can becomes a shield, a tricycle is a "supersonic war bike," and a tire swing serves as an "anti-gravity, solar-powered planet hopper." Even their pets assume important roles, and a wandering butterfly becomes the White Wizard.

The backyard offers them a wonderful, expansive place where their voices can rise and spirits can soar. There is no need for them to be cautious, to hold back, and think small. As they become immersed in their fantasy, the two feel more and more exhilarated, constantly sparking each other, taking it further, and entering deeper.

When imaginative thinkers pool their resources, they have the power to create something new and extraordinary. It may be a spaceship like Imagination I (Keats) or a special and intriguing world like Roxaboxen (McLerran) or Terabithia (Paterson). These collaborators learn to trust and play off each other while forming magical alliances.

Costume play permits children safely to become other beings and cultivate their own style. Materials can speak to and inspire children in an intuitive way. The elements of color, texture, size, and shape may suggest an array of possibilities. With a mere scrap of cloth and a slight change in voice and body movement, children can bring to life new and vibrant characters. A piece of fabric can be transformed into an old woman's shawl, a prince's turban, a matador's cape.

When Max in *Where the Wild Things Are* (Sendak) puts on his wolf suit, he becomes the boisterous, "dare me" boy with the big roar. Exiled to his room for flaunting his attitude, he sails to the Land of Wild Things, proclaims himself king, and orders the "wild rumpus" to begin. The simple act of wearing a costume helps stimulate his fantasies and empowers him to be commanding and comically defiant. It also enables him to channel his anger and aggression.

Another Sendak character is Rosie, the spark of her neighborhood and leader of the Nutshell Kids. In fact, she dresses to the nines with definite flair and mock elegance, wearing a brown-feathered hat, oversized red gown, elbow-length gloves, a boa, and blue high heels. With grand dreams, shrewdness, and very little modesty, Rosie organizes and directs others to perform in a movie about her life. Both Rosie and Max are buoyed by what they are wearing, and their costumes surely contribute to their outrageousness.

Many children have a favorite costume or item of clothing. The unconventional Jennie in *Jennie's Hat* (Keats) derives pleasure from wearing hats and experiments with a straw basket, TV antenna, and metal cooking pan. What can she do to embellish the plain Sunday hat she has received from her favorite aunt? How can she make it striking and original?

Even more passionate is the girl obsessed with earrings in Judith Viorst's witty and lively picture book of the same name. This child has a medley of compelling reasons for getting her ears pierced. Demonstrative, single-minded, and unbridled in her enthusiasm, she is both charming and willful and perhaps a parent's nightmare.

The little boy in *I Wish I Had a Pirate Suit* (Allen) dreams of owning a pirate costume so that he will be the captain instead of his older brother. He is tired of being the entire rest of the crew and cannot wait to call the shots and partake in the plunder of fake gold and jelly bellies.

Spontaneous costume play can take place anywhere—in an attic or yard, school dress-up corner, or pediatric playroom. Masks, wigs, headbands, and robes can stimulate and sustain hours of make-believe. This kind of play involves children trying out various roles and apparel and improvising dialogue as their dramas unfold. Shy children are free to be feisty and bold, and more robust children can try out quieter modes of behavior. Any child can play at being any age or either gender without being judged.

More formalized roleplaying may entail children developing a play and performing it for others. Costumes serve to animate a character and accentuate certain qualities and may be simple and fluid or elaborate and detailed.

Children who shy away from dramatic play may still invest care and imagination when making a costume for Halloween, Purim, Three Kings Day, or other holiday celebrations. Just trick-or-treating or walking in a parade can be liberating for children who do not always feel free to express their individuality and spirit.

Costumes help create mood and texture, linking child and culture, old world and new world. Striking icons and symbols reflecting a group's history and values often dominate a particular event. An eager Ernie Wan prepares for his new role as Lion Dancer (Waters and Slovenz-Low) for Chinese New Year in New York City's Chinatown. Carefully, he examines the lion's head. Do the ears wiggle? Do the eyes blink? On that night, will Ernie dance with force and grace and "bring honor to his family"?

In *Vejigante* (Delacre), Ramon, a Puerto Rican boy, realizes his dream when he is old enough to become a masquerader at Carnival. Excitedly, he works to complete his papier-mâché horned mask and a shaker made from an inflated cow's bladder. In his black-and-white goat-like costume, he will be able to pull off pranks and tease the spirits. His concealed identity gives him a freedom and secret power. At last he will truly be part of his culture. He might even be noticed by the bigger guys and make an impression on their leader, El Gallo.

Dressing up a snowman or a scarecrow can also challenge children to be inventive and stylish, to play with colors, and to experiment with materials. Bric-a-brac, burlap, ribbons, and felt can become highly valued ingredients. One unusual touch, vivid detail, or exaggerated feature can make a creation stand out and help give it character. Such is the case in *The Black Snowman* (Mendez) when two brothers drape their "sooty" snowman with a frayed yet colorful cloth. The newly found kente proves to be a powerful fabric, and their feelings about their blackness and African heritage are soon to be altered forever.

Any costume, whether homemade or bought, can free a child from certain anxieties and inhibitions. The costume becomes a passport for taking risks, trying out new identities, playmaking and bonding with peers, and, on special occasions, for hobnobbing with beasties, ghouls, and creatures of the night.

> I'm a timid brave on a wooded hill
> Where demons dance, and the winds bring chill.
>
> I am a swallow learning to glide
> Bursting and thumping and tingling inside.
>
> I'm a newborn shadow thinking about
> How to be silent and when to come out.

I'm a butterfly! I'm a balloon!
I spin and create in my thoughtful cocoon.

Creative Excursions

The Magical Mini-Drama.   One way to encourage children to extend their imagination is to engage them in the process of creating mini-dramas. Working in pairs, children could develop improvised scenes tied to particular themes. With younger children, these scenes could be based on the content of picture books. For example, the first mini-drama suggested, "At the Zoo" (see below), could be used after reading *The Escape of Marvin the Ape* (Buehner). The fifth mini-drama, "Secret Worlds" (see below), could be used as a way to extend *The Tub People* (Conrad).

Each mini-drama might last from one minute to four or five minutes. If they choose, children could be allowed to use a few simple props or costume pieces—perhaps a hat, some kind of fabric, a mask, or a walking stick. Certain pairs of children might want to exchange roles and try their encounter a second time.

What is important is that the players seem real and believable and have a clear sense of their situation and context. They need to know what their character is thinking and feeling when the improvisation begins. After each mini-drama, others might want to share their observations.

This activity can be used as a way of animating or extending a story. It can stimulate creative writing or initiate a unit of study. A particular mini-drama could be developed into a longer improvised play in which a character resolves a conflict or journeys to a magical world.

Through this kind of experience, children are permitted to be other selves. They learn to think quickly and listen carefully and are encouraged to express their poetry and feelings.

The following are suggestions for mini-dramas. In each situation, one child is given a specific role, and the second child is free to create a character that the first character might encounter. After the scene, other children may want to enter as well.

At the Zoo.   You are a tough and grouchy detective. You have been called in to investigate how the gorilla escaped from the zoo. You never crack a smile, but you always crack the case. Who might you encounter? Some possibilities:

• A giraffe that was not paying attention because she was having an ugly neck ache.
• A monkey that does not know a thing because he was practicing his guitar.
• A polar bear that was busy lifting weights.
• A baboon that was signing autographs.
• A snake that was involved in a hissing contest.

The Partygoer.   You have been invited to a party. As you enter, what you see is eerie and chilling. There are no other children, only characters from scary movies. But you are unafraid and eager to meet these unusual guests. Who do you encounter? Some possibilities:

- A lady vampire who is allergic to blood.
- A timid wolfman who is trying to develop a heart-thumping howl.
- Mrs. Mummy who can only moan and groan.
- A dancing ogre who tries to teach you "The Monster Rag."

The Real Estate Agent. You are trying to entice buyers to buy one of the vacant homes in the Fairy-Tale Kingdom, and you always come up with good selling points. Who do you encounter? Some possibilities:

- Someone interested in the Old Woman's Shoe.
- Someone interested in the First Pig's House of Straw.
- Someone interested in Rapunzel's Tower.
- Someone interested in Sleeping Beauty's Castle.

Earth Kite. You charge across the park, holding your kite up to dazzle the wind. But the wind is not very impressed, and your kite falls flatly to the ground. You try again, and still you fail. This makes you angry, and you look for someone to help you. Who do you encounter? Some possibilities:

- A bullying boxer who thinks you should use scare tactics.
- A banker who thinks you should promise your kite a savings account.
- A pilot who says the problem rests in the tail. He helps you extend it with some pieces of cloth.
- A witch who thinks flying the kite depends on the spirits, and she helps you mix a brew and recite a chant.

Secret Worlds. You are a reporter for the Fantasy Press. You wish to write a story about the tiny, magical people who live in odd and offbeat places. Who might you interview? Some possibilities:

- One of the tub people who are riding on a bar of soap.
- One of the stomach people who are inspecting a midnight snack.
- One of the clock people who are playing tricks with the time.
- One of the cloud people who are suffering from the polluted air.
- One of the conch people who are trying to sweep out the sand in her home with a seagull feather.

Pink Lemonade. You have opened your lemonade stand. It is elegant. You are using cups of china. You even have a silk tablecloth and a fancy gold guest book for your customers to sign. You expect to earn a lot of money because you have picked a perfect spot on a perfectly humid day. Who do you encounter? Some possibilities:

- A man on a horse with an urgent look on his face. He warns you that the Redcoats are coming.

- An extremely old man with a cane and a beard. He is trying to construct a boat and keeps talking about a flood.
- A flustered girl who is worried about being late. She keeps talking about a white rabbit and some sort of tea party.
- A thirsty boy who wants to pay you with a magic bean. He says he sold his cow for three of them.

The Park Bench.   You are sitting on a park bench, feeling very relaxed and peaceful as you read your Sunday newspaper. You cherish these moments, but things are about to change. Who do you encounter? Some possibilities:

- An energetic actor rehearsing all the parts of a melodrama.
- A politician lecturing on her soapbox.
- A cheerleader practicing for a pep rally.
- A persistent peddler with a cart of lotions and potions.
- An exasperated butterfly catcher trying out his new net.
- A little man with a guitar serenading the squirrels in a nearby tree.

The Tollbooth.   You are a tollbooth worker and must deal every day with travelers in need of directions. Some travelers refuse to pay or have no change. But most are pleasant and cooperative and like to talk about their vehicles. Who do you encounter? Some possibilities:

- Mr. Toad in his Model T.
- Farmer Palmer in his wagon.
- The Stone Goblin on his bicycle.
- Miss Gulch on her bicycle.
- Ralph E. Mouse on his motorcycle.
- The Ox-Cart Man.
- Fantastic Mr. Fox with his wheelbarrow.
- Colin in his wheelchair.
- The White Witch on her sled.
- Cinderella in her coach.
- James in his peach-mobile.
- Milo in his electric car.

The Insect Problem Center.   You are a counselor at the Insect Problem Center, a busy and important place where insects come to work out their problems. It is your job to listen and to help them find solutions. Who do you encounter? Some possibilities:

- A firefly with a dimming beam.
- A cricket that would like to change to the day shift.

- An annoying mosquito that wants to make a better impression on others.
- An ill-mannered ladybug that wants to improve her etiquette.
- An eager ant seeking advice on how to raid a picnic. ("Do you go after the potato salad first?")
- A flea from a flea circus that wants help on how to organize a union. ("We need nets, insurance, better benefits.")
- A caterpillar that is anxious about becoming a butterfly. ("I like the low life—the moss and the grass. I don't want to be high up, getting dizzy and bumping into tree thorns.")

The Squire's Journey.   You are a lonely, loyal squire and have been searching for your knight. You wander around the countryside, asking questions and observing everything. Who do you encounter? Some possibilities:

- A professional dragon-slayer who wants to give you lessons.
- An autograph seeker with quill and ink who shows you Merlin's signature. ("Now if I could just get Guinevere's.")
- A spirited girl who has run away from Fair Maiden School.
- A court jester who is desperate to find some funnier routines.
- The queen's chef who is on a quest for rare and delectable herbs.
- A herald who is practicing proclamations.
- A retired beast-master reminiscing about his marvelous unicorn.

....

I came from very far away, and I've traveled even farther. I am a squire, and I've been searching for my knight for seven long and weary years. I've met many and learned much. For instance, there was the time I met a very sore-throated dragon. I'll never forget the way his eyes kept sizing me up. And then there was that nervous little old carpenter. You see he had to build a round table, rounder than the bottom of a barrel, and he hadn't the faintest idea how. I hope he got it all right in the end. A task like that is very trying on one's patience.

Max Kuemmerlein, age 14

....

The Scrap and Boa Shop.   In this make-believe shop, pairs of younger and middle-grade children can choose three or four items from among crowns, masks, robes, feather boas, and fabric pieces in order to develop characters and short, improvised scenes. These dramatic encounters, to be shared with others, might involve a peddler, the Patchwork Pirate, the Garment Queen, the Commissioner of Rags, the Minister of Muffs, or the Secretary of Silks.

The Hatbox Theater.   Small groups of younger and middle-grade children could develop improvised plays using hats that suggest characters and situations.

The Court Jester, from "The Squire's Journey." Illustrated by Paul Kuemmerlein, age 13.

A hat itself might be at the pivotal heart of each drama. For example, a hat collector covets a gardener's golden-flowered sun hat; a warlock loses his psychic powers when his long-pointed crimson hat disappears. The actors might choose hats from the hatbox or create hats of their own. These might include a Western hat, a beanie, a cap, a crown, Haman's three-cornered hat, versions of Aunt

The Sore-Throated Dragon, from "The Squire's Journey." Illustrated by Paul Kuemmerlein.

Flossie's (Howard), Uncle Nacho's (Rohmer), or the Quangle-Wangle's (Lear) hats, or a fanciful bonnet with a kite or a nest on the top.

A Miniature Scarecrow Park. The sensitive friendship tale *The Scarebird* (Fleischman) or the whimsical *Barn Dance!* (Martin, Jr., and Archambault) might inspire middle-grade children to create a model park of miniature scarecrows with straw, sticks, cloth, pipe cleaners, buttons, etc. The scarecrows might include an astronomer, bird-watcher, chef, circus performer, football player, and opera singer. Some children might wish to create a picture book about the adventures of their straw person.

A Costume Design Club. Interested older children might collaborate on a sketchbook and design costumes for famous literary characters–the Rough-Face Girl, Harlequin, the heroine from *Moss Gown* (Hooks), the Mad Hatter and the March Hare, Miss Nelson and Viola Swamp. Some children might create a costume book that features folktale characters going to a coronation, wedding, or masquerade ball.

The Herald, from "The Squire's Journey." Illustrated by Paul Kuemmerlein.

A Villains' Fashion Parade. Older children might design, make costumes, and then appear in the Great Villains' Fashion Parade. A narrator can describe the traits and wicked deeds of each strutting villain, and these might include Cruella De Vil, Miss Hannigan, Loki, Moriarity, and Catwoman. Each villain, in turn, could share his or her fashion tips.

The Power of Masks Exhibit. Older children could design and develop an exhibit that illustrates the power and universality of masks. How are the masks constructed? Why are they important in rituals and ceremonies? How might they be used for healing? How are they incorporated into certain kinds of theater and dance? Children could display masks from many cultures, playful

"Scarecrow Park." Illustrated by Max Kuemmerlein, age 14.

carnival masks, and masks that are fierce and unsettling. They can add a dramatic dimension to the exhibit by presenting an original play about a mask maker or performing scenes from *The Phantom of the Opera* (Leroux) or *The Masque of the Red Death* (Poe).

Thump Theater. Children of all ages could develop improvised scenes in which the sound of "thump" sets the tone and begins the action. A scene, for example, might involve a doctor listening to someone's heartbeat. Each mini-drama must begin with the clear sound of "thump" repeated three or four times.
   Possible scenarios for "thump" plays:

- A drum beats slowly as the messenger of the Gnome-King calls all forest gnomes together to announce something important.
- Two bragging beavers use their tails to engage in a thumping contest to see which of them can make the loudest sound.

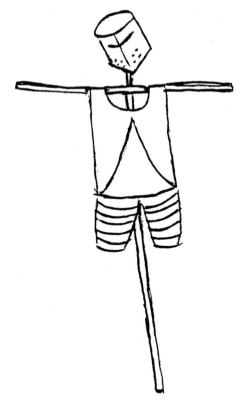

"Scarecrow Park." Illustrated by Max Kuemmerlein.

- An anguished giant paces through his domain, wondering who has stolen his silver-engraved yo-yo.
- A woodcutter cuts down three enchanted fig trees in order to break a sorcerer's spell.

Possible scenarios for "snap" plays:

- The king's pea snapper has over 300 pods to go in order to make the royal pea soup.
- A bossy, mean-tempered snapdragon stirs up trouble in the garden.
- A frustrated photographer cannot get a family to stay still and stop bickering.
- An annoyed girl keeps snapping for her genie, and her genie always has excuses for being late.

Possible scenarios for "squeak" plays:

- The Field Mouse Choir rehearses the Cheese Cantata but the director is not very pleased.
- A tour guide insists on absolute quiet as the group proceeds through the Museum of Silence, but one child's new shoes keep squeaking.

- Two children discover a swing in a deserted playground that keeps moving back and forth, but no one appears to be on it.

Teach Me! Toad School by Cathy Bellows could inspire children to create improvisations about teaching and learning. Working in pairs, the child who is the instructor would be given a specific role and situation (the other player would be the student). Some possibilities:

- You are a mother spider teaching your son how to spin a web.
- You are a ladybug stressing to your daughter the importance of manners before she goes out into the world.
- You are a shadow teaching a newborn shadow about his job. You tell him when in the day he can come out. You explain to him how to move silently and how to keep a secret.
- You are a clown teaching a beginner about your art. You show her how to walk and fall and put on makeup. You explain to her the secret of what makes people laugh.
- You are a mother mouse grimly explaining to your son what a cat is. You describe the sharpness of its teeth and the power of its claws. You are trying hard to leave an impression.
- You are a professor at the Pirate Academy teaching a student how to swab the deck, dress in pirate fashion, and say "Shiver me timbers!"
- You are an instructor at Camelot College teaching an eager young knight about doing good deeds.
- You are an exasperated chef at Strega Nona's School of Pasta Making, and you are having difficulties with a student named Big Anthony.
- You are teaching a complicated routine at the Ballet School for Gorillas.

Shoe Box Stages. Children, after selecting a story to dramatize, could create puppet theaters out of shoe boxes, in pairs or in small groups. First, the lids are removed and boxes are placed on their sides. A slot is cut on the top of the box, so that the paper or oak tag puppets can come down through the top. Popsicle sticks can be glued on the back of the puppet heads so that the puppets can be manipulated. Children would also need to make one or two backgrounds out of construction paper that would fit inside the boxes. Some children might want to use tabs to create three-dimensional objects on their stages such as a cactus, giant flower, rock, or tree stump. Some may wish to devise a way of making curtains.

The following picture books are excellent springboards for launching this kind of project.

The Native American trickster tale *Raven* (McDermott) can excite children to create a new trickster–either a person or animal–and a series of humorous episodes.

The Rough-Face Girl (Martin, R.) is an Algonquin version of the Cinderella story in which the heroine is wise and resourceful, taking matters into her own hands. Children could create puppet plays about other folktale heroines.

The Thieves' Market (Haseley) might entice children to create puppet plays that occur in the marketplace—a world of beggars, buyers, merchants, and entertainers.

Mrs. Vinegar (Stern), whose residence is a glass bottle, until a spring-cleaning mishap causes her to move, might stimulate children to create puppet plays about the tiny people who live in unusual places. The water-lily people, for example, might share their lily pads with some amiable frogs, and spend a few hours each day bottling fragrance drops from the lilies, which they sell as perfume. Other puppet plays might involve people who live in a bakery, baseball dugout, chimney, old shipyard, lighthouse, or the prop room of a theater.

Similarly, *The Wing Shop* (Woodruff) could inspire children to make puppet plays that take place in some unusual kind of shop. For example, at the Sparkle Shop, one might find all the shiniest things: jewels, gold buttons, and glitter. At the Hair and Wig Shop, the customers might include Medusa and Rapunzel. At the Invention Shop, one might discover a one-hour bubble.

After the shoe-box stages and puppets have been created, children can practice their plays and then perform them for each other, present them to younger children, or share them at a senior center.

Resources

Books

Allen, Pamela. *I Wish I Had a Pirate Suit*. Viking, 1990.

Bailie, Allan. *Drac and the Gremlin*. Dial, 1989.

Bellows, Cathy. *Toad School*. Atheneum, 1990.

Buehner, Carolyn. *The Escape of Marvin the Ape*. Puffin, 1999.

Conrad, Pam. *The Tub People*. Laura Geringer, 1989.

Delacre, Lulu. *Vejigante*. Scholastic, 1993.

Fleischman, Sid. *The Scarebird*. Mulberry, 1994.

Haseley, Dennis. *The Thieves' Market*. HarperCollins, 1991.

Hoffman, Mary. *Amazing Grace*. Dial, 1981.

Hooks, William. *Moss Gown*. Clarion, 1987.

Howard, Elizabeth. *Aunt Flossie's Hats and Crabcakes Later*. Clarion, 1991.

Keats, Ezra Jack. *Jennie's Hat*. Harper, 1985.

Lear, Edward. *The Quangle-Wangle's Hat*. Harcourt, 1988.

Martin, Jr., Bill, and Archambault, John. *Barn Dance!* Holt, 1986.

Martin, Rafe. *The Rough-Face Girl*. Putnam, 1992.

McDermott, Gerald. *Raven: A Trickster Tale from the Pacific Northwest*. Harcourt, 1993.

Mendez, Phil. *The Black Snowman*. Scholastic, 1989.

Rohmer, Harriet. *Uncle Nacho's Hat*. Children's Book Press, 1989.

Sendak, Maurice. *Maurice Sendak's Really Rosie*. Harper, 1975.

Sendak, Maurice. *Where the Wild Things Are*. Harper, 1963.

Stern, Simon. *Mrs. Vinegar*. Prentice, 1979.

Thomson, Sarah L. *Imagine a Day*. Atheneum, 2005.

Viorst, Judith. *Earrings*. Atheneum, 1990.

Waters, Kate, and Slovenz-Low, Madeline. *Lion Dancer*. Scholastic, 1990.

Willard, Nancy. *The Nightgown of the Sullen Moon*. Harcourt, 1983.

Woodruff, Elvira. *The Wing Shop*. Holiday, 1991.

Films, Videos, and DVDs

Really Rosie. Sheriss, 1976. 26 minutes.

THEME 5:
Neighborhood Jams ·· ●

Open windows and whirling fans help relieve the sticky weather for apartment dwellers in Eleanor Schick's *One Summer Night*. A girl named Laura, dancing to a record, becomes the catalyst for a neighborhood jam. Soon the rhythmic sounds permeate throughout the block and everyone is moving to the music, some with drums, others with spoons. Oh, what an infectious tale this is—one that captures the carnival spirit of a neighborhood in harmony.

Any number of words might be used to describe a neighborhood: "turf," "territory," "reservation," "suburb," "El Barrio," "ashram," "village," "township," or "community." What defines a neighborhood? Are its boundaries clear and imposing, or vague and forever in flux? How do neighborhoods evolve, and why do they sometimes die and disappear?

For children, the neighborhood is all-encompassing—a universe of its own, an on-the-spot academy, an organic theater where street vignettes offer a spectrum of human dramas. Each child's sense of "neighborhood" is personal and varied. Some neighborhoods are wondrous, vibrant, and flourishing, while others may be seen as bleak, decaying, and confining. Each one, though, has its distinctiveness, its particular "feel" and "look" and "sound." Each has its people who give it heart, color, character, and humanity. Each has its history and lore, its episodes and tales, often embellished, which surface time and again.

Within neighborhoods are special places that infuse it with energy and good vibrations. Places such as a recreation center, community garden, or public library may generate activity and excitement and foster fellowship and the spirit of exchange. In contrast, there are also scary places like condemned buildings and alleyways that seem to haunt children, entering their fantasies and dreams.

A Neighborhood Roundup

A number of books and films can provide children with glimpses of neighborhood life around the globe. How would one describe these worlds? Do the people who live there feel a security and sense of belonging?

Carrie's multicultural neighborhood in *Everybody Cooks Rice* (Dooley) is a close-knit and welcoming place where the smell of spices drifts out of each home. As she goes door-to-door, looking for her brother, she samples rice dishes from Barbados, Vietnam, India, China, and Haiti.

Jafta (Lewin), who lives in a South African village, has access to a rich variety of plant and animal life—baobab and blue gum trees, lizards and impalas. He engages in a series of events: a harvest, a wedding, and a freedom rally, but all the time he is missing his father. What happens to the men in his village, and why are they being pulled away from their homes?

Naomi's Amish world in *Just Plain Fancy* (Polacco) is peaceful, rural, communal—a world of washhouses and horse-drawn buggies. When Naomi, who takes care of the chickens, becomes attached to a "fancy" young bird with bright colors, does she risk being shunned for wanting a pet that is anything but "plain"?

Certain books depict neighborhoods in other times, paying careful attention to accuracy and detail. Peppe's "bustling" neighborhood in *Peppe the Lamplighter* (Bartone) is Little Italy in New York City at the turn of the century. His is a neighborhood of tenements, of peddlers and pushcarts. Peppe is pleased with his temporary job, subbing for the lamplighter. As he sets each lamp aflame, he makes a wish for each member of his family. This ritual empowers him, and he loves controlling the light and illuminating the dark.

The suburban London neighborhood evoked in the film *Hope and Glory* is in tumult and chaos, caught in the blitz of World War II. Air-raid sirens become part of the soundscape, and every moment is fraught with peril and adventure. Billy, the film's 9-year-old hero, feels freed by the experience—relishing the unknown, the unexpected humor, the helter-skelter quality of each day. With routines disrupted and abandoned, he can roam around with his band of friends, exploring a world of new possibilities. Together, under fiery skies, they search for treasured pieces of shrapnel and have little time to be bored.

Neighborhoods in Harmony

What brings the people of any neighborhood together? Are there common values? Are there certain shared pleasures and festivities like block parties, barn raisings, Halloween parades, and harvest dances? Some neighborhoods are resonant with people coming together in productive ways—organizing a recycling project, building a tower of junk, or repairing a playground. How might individuals restore pride in neighborhoods starting to deteriorate? How might a crisis—a blizzard, flood, fire, or tornado—demand the mutual support of people and test their resilience?

Harlem, 1957, as rendered in *Irene and the Big Fine Nickel* (Smalls-Hector), is a neighborhood with a welcoming spirit. Irene and her friends feel very protected here, whether making a box garden on the fire escape or sharing raisin buns on the curb. In fact, Irene knows the names of all the people who work in the stores.

The ambitious boy in the film *Santiago's Ark* learns he can count on others after constructing a boat on his tenement roof. How will he get his boat to the water, and how do his neighbors come through for him?

Many times, the reaching out in neighborhoods is manifested in the one-to-one moments of private encounters. Such is the case in *Wilfred Gordon McDonald Partridge* (Fox), about a boy who lives next door to a nursing home. His favorite person there, Miss Nancy Alison Delacourt Cooper, has four names just as he does. When disease threatens her memory, he brings her a shoe box of treasures—tangible, tactile things like seashells and a "fresh warm egg." He wishes to stir her feelings and thoughts and to reconnect her to her childhood. These two, despite the age difference, are indeed the best of neighbors.

Most neighborhoods have gathering places where children come to socialize and engage in both sports and quiet activities. Hangouts are sometimes private and unsupervised by adults. They may take the form of a village square, vacant lot, clubhouse, park, meadow, mall, candy store, video arcade, or someone's backyard. In many areas, the pizza shop has come to function as the child's version of an English pub.

Neighborhoods also have planned events that can stimulate social interaction and foster feelings of harmony. These include barbecues, block parties, rent parties, carnivals, concerts, rummage sales, kite festivals, firework displays, clean-up and recycling days, and fancy premieres at the local movie house with speakers blaring and spotlights shining.

In *The Walking Catfish* (Day), neighbors gather at Gunther's General Store for the big, three-day Lie Contest. The bang of a hammer on a cracker barrel begins the fantastical yarn spinning, and the "air is so blue with lies you can hardly see the other side of the store." This is a community that values the oral tradition, in particular, the tall tale and whopper. Even children are inspired to be flavorful and outrageous with words, to twist the truth and imagine the impossible.

The heart of some neighborhoods is the marketplace. Children may be fascinated by the street merchants—about their persuasive words and colorful displays and where they go when the workday ends.

What draws a child to a particular item? How does he or she decide on just one thing when there are so many enticing choices? In *Zamani Goes to Market* (Feelings), Zamani is rewarded with two coins for watching over the family's brown calf. Now that he has a little purchasing power, what should he buy? Should it be something for himself or a gift for a loved one? He examines the ornaments, the straw hats, and the "bead-covered gourds." He knows he must be patient and not impulsive, for he wants to feel grown-up and make a wise decision.

Maybe he could buy his first kanzu, the one with the "orange braid around the collar," or should he consider a striking head necklace for his mother? This proud African boy has a lot of pondering to do and is feeling very torn.

In a St. Louis neighborhood in the 1930s, people gather around the medicine wagon to hear the medicine man hustle his many tonics, potions, and powders—special remedies in colorful bottles. When evening comes, he announces a dance contest and the prize of a silver dollar for the winner.

Despite her young age and small size, a girl named Ragtime Tumpie (Schroeder) begs to enter, and the medicine man obliges. Soon this barefoot girl is enchanting the audience with her air of confidence, amazing footwork, and infectious joy. The sounds from a harmonica and fiddle help to create the ragtime beat, and kerosene torches provide all the light that is needed. Tumpie is a natural, a pure and genuine talent. She owns the stage, and the silver dollar is hers.

In this true neighborhood story, the medicine man is the encouraging one, the show maker, the man who makes possible a truly magical night. In fact, this is the night when Ragtime Tumpie first proclaims that she will someday be a dancer. Later in life, she will be known throughout the world as Josephine Baker.

The Carnival Is Coming!

For some children, the highlight of each summer is when the carnival sets up in their neighborhood or community. No doubt they are lured by the dazzle of lights, the rinky-dink rhythms, and the wheels of all sizes whirling in motion. A world in itself, the carnival is a place for the unexpected—irresistible and intoxicating, tacky and sublime. It allows children to perform physical feats and prove their mastery as they win all types of games and prizes.

The carnival appeals to all of their senses with its vibrant colors, sweet and spicy flavors, and catchy calliope tunes. Children may react in a myriad of ways. They may feel overstimulated, euphoric, or as if they are spinning out of control. Some will experience a rush, a sense of surrendering and being carried away. Questions and concerns may dance around and then disappear. "Who will I meet here?" "What might I win?" "Is the snake woman real or fake?" "Can I eat a whole foot-long hot dog all by myself?" "Why does this magical day ever have to end?"

Anything can happen here. Punch and Judy may delight children with their nonstop sparring. West Indian paraders may enchant them with their brightly feathered costumes. Out of nowhere, a lion dancer might appear, or Queen Esther, or someone with a familiar voice wearing a Vejigante mask. The Red Knight and his squire might be sandwiching at the very next table.

Simply going to the carnival nourishes friendships as well, as pairs and small groups wander about—giggling, preening, commenting on the scene, being terrified together on the Lightning Loop or the Scream Machine. Excitedly, yet cautiously, they survey all the wild and rickety rides—rides that jerk and loop and speed and tilt.

A carnival may also have its dark side—freakish, intriguing, mysterious. Children may be drawn to the sideshows and all their bizarre attractions. How, in defining the world, do they make sense of the Fungus Man or the Slime Lady? What is authentic, and what is illusion? Why might some children find these encounters to be unsettling?

For Wheel Wiggins, in *Big Wheel* (Singer), putting together a carnival to win a Fourth of July best-celebration contest teaches him a few lessons in leadership. As the guy with big ideas and as the creative catalyst for his gang, Wheel is overly invested in this project, flirting with tyranny and forgetting, at times, how to nurture the ideas and strengths of his friends. His grand vision of a Western-flavored daredevil and magic show begins to elude him when he becomes too much the taskmaster.

Ultimately, he is able to admit his mistakes and learn something about when or when not to listen to the advice of others. This humorous story illustrates how a carnival can stimulate children's inventiveness and encourage collaboration.

Neighborhoods in Conflict

What sets neighbors apart? How do conflicts and feuds foster divisiveness? What happens when a family is ostracized because of religion or race, or because one of its members has AIDS? How do poverty, drugs, and gangs chip away at the soul of a community and create pockets of friction and despair?

The Araboolies of Liberty Street (Swope) is a witty fable about conformity. It involves an eccentric new family that arrives on the block. Among other things, they do not speak English and have the nerve to sleep on the lawn in one, giant-sized bed.

In *The Widow's Broom* (Van Allsburg), Minna Shaw's neighbors react harshly and violently to her broom with special powers—a broom that can sweep by itself and tap tunes on the piano. They are seized with suspicion and fear over something that is "strange" and "different."

The exuberant David in *Pumpkinseeds* (Yezback) wishes to share his bag of treats with others, but his neighbors ignore him and brush him away with a "We're not supposed to talk to strangers." This sprightly boy, undismayed, crushes the seeds and then scatters them for the birds.

In any neighborhood when conflicts arise, individuals may emerge to break through the tension and rekindle in others a sense of tolerance. Billy, in *Billy the Great* (Guy), is warm and inclusive. He does not prejudge others and is able to dispel the anger his parents feel toward their neighbors. A second peacemaker is Maniac Magee (Spinelli). Compassionate and wise, he rejects his town's rigid boundaries. His friendships transcend geography and color, and he travels freely through both parts of town, appreciating the humor and generosity he finds in both worlds.

Sometimes a neighborhood crowd can become a collective bully, especially when those in control have scary and destructive agendas. Certain members of the group may feel confused and conflicted—torn between their need to conform and their own buried decency.

In *Circle of Fire* (Hooks), Harrison Hawkins, an 11-year-old, secretly witnesses a gathering of ghost-like figures in front of a flaming cross. He is repelled by this sight of Klansmen terrorizing gypsies with shotguns and "leather snake" bullwhips. For a long time, he feels helpless and overwhelmed. What can he do? How can he stop this violence from happening?

In *To Kill a Mockingbird* (Lee), Scout Finch watches cautiously as "sullen looking, sleepy eyed men" try to push their way into the Maycomb town jail. They are trying to lynch a black man, Tom Robbins, but are thwarted by Scout's father, Atticus, sitting firmly and resolutely in front of the door.

This murmuring half-circle festers with malice and rage, and everyone is extremely tense. Luckily, Scout recognizes one of the men and begins chatting away with her usual warmth and directness. "Hey, Mr. Cunningham. I go to school with Walter. He's your boy, ain't he?"

With this conversation starter, Scout punctures the mood and turns things around. Her good instincts defuse a desperate situation, and the people, no longer faceless or anonymous, disperse and return to their homes.

The Neighborhood as a Memory Place

The neighborhood can become a memory place filled with haunting details and bittersweet moments. Children may move away from the neighborhood, but the images are internalized and carried for a lifetime—perhaps images of polished marble steps, a Kool-Aid stand, a go-cart race, a paper route, Mr. Softee, a tire swing, a vicious dog, or a few old men playing dominos.

Some things, filtered through time, become distorted, enlarged, romanticized. *I Remember "121"* (Haskins) and *Long Ago in Oregon* (Lewis) bring to life specific worlds, looking back from an adult perspective. Bill Cosby, through storytelling, recalls his brushes with "trouble" and his mischievous ways, growing up with Fat Albert and friends in Philadelphia.

Gary Soto's *Neighborhood Odes* celebrates his Mexican American neighborhood in Fresno, California. He offers poetic tributes to snow cones, sprinklers, tortillas, and mariachis. His odes reveal his fear of La Lorone, "a woman dripping water in July when no rain has fallen," and his pride in the local two-room library. He even rhapsodizes over his friend Pablo's "rain beaten, sun beaten" sneakers. His language is always exuberant, crackling, and musical—much like the world he has re-created.

Creative Excursions

Animated Neighborhood Maps. Younger children, individually or in pairs, can make animated, three-dimensional maps of their neighborhood with parts that pop up. The maps would highlight the location of important sites as seen from their perspective. These personal landmarks might include the best pizza shop and the best hill for sliding, the headquarters of the Spy Club, the church where the carnival is held, the empty lot that for one week became a movie set, and the places to avoid on Halloween night.

The Playground Sketchbook. Younger children could visit a neighborhood playground as observers with pencils and sketchpad and create drawings of playground life. They might focus on a balloon man sculpting animals or an incident taking place at the drinking fountain. The drawings could be compiled into a playground sketchbook.

A Moving, Breathing Playground. This is a pantomime activity. Children, using only their bodies, would have to create the different playground attractions. How might they create the merry-go-round or the jungle gym? How might they simulate the movement of the seesaw, the swing, or the slide? They could also bring to life some of the playground people—the vendors, park performers, marble-shooters, jump ropers, hopscotch players, roller skaters, and skateboarders. At some point, children could add sounds.

An Ezra Keats Festival. Ezra Keats wrote with simplicity and charm about the everyday dramas of neighborhood children, and his characters are imaginative, boundless, and resourceful—often creating things out of limited materials. Younger children could celebrate this author/illustrator by inviting others to join them in a festival of story-inspired activities. During this special event, some children could draw a cityscape emphasizing windows, fire escapes, stoops and steps, even the graffiti on buildings and fences. Some could make a collage of a neighborhood scene or a shoe-box world like the one that Louie creates in *The Trip*. Others may want to illustrate their dreams with crayons on the "dream wall" as a way of remembering Roberto and the night he could not fall asleep (see *Dreams*). There could also be special booths or areas where children could take a "pretend" trip to the moon on Imagination II, enter their pets in the Pet Show, or create Styrofoam "snow people" in honor of *The Snowy Day*.

Pretzel Girl. Middle-grade children might want to develop a comic strip, accordion book, flip book, short animated film, or video about a heroic character that is the true protector of the neighborhood playground. For example, imagine a character named Pretzel Girl fighting for playground fairness and justice. She is a peacemaker, troubleshooter, negotiator, and problem solver. At any time, she may have to deal with someone who cuts in line at the drinking fountain, hogs the base, or throws litter on the ground. Wearing a brown cape and a shirt with a big "P" on it, she likes to sit in the pretzel position and is always sharing her salty snack with others. What is Pretzel Girl's real identity? Why is she so motivated to prevent playground crime, and how did Henrietta, the hot dog vendor, become her archenemy?

The Street Merchants' Mural. The brightly colored paintings in *A Street Called Home* (Robinson) and the lush, exquisite watercolors in *Caribbean Canvas* (Lessac) could inspire middle-grade children to develop a mural of a street market in which each child creates one of the vendors and his or her wares.

A Merchant's Lament. Middle-grade children, pretending to be street merchants, could write poems or narratives that express their complaints, concerns, frustrations, and fears.

A Merchant's Rewards. Middle-grade children, pretending to be street merchants, could write poems or narratives that express their joys and delights, the moments that are humorous, and the moments that are the most satisfying.

The Pitch. Middle-grade children could become peddlers and vendors at a neighborhood marketplace. They need to be clever and persuasive as they take turns trying to sell a phony tonic (one that can prevent both baldness and beestings), a new invention (a toy enlarger or smell collector), or a historical item (maybe a silver goblet from Nero's time or an authentic Colonial calendar).

The Neighborhood Stock Company. Every neighborhood has a vivid gallery of characters who enrich the surroundings and may be remembered by others for a lifetime. There might be the eccentric Miss Orange, who dresses in only one color and even has orange shoes; the Growling Man, who barks if you wander too near his yard; or Mysterious Marv, who carries a huge burlap bag and speaks most of the time in riddles. *Rolling Harvey Down the Hill* (Prelutsky), which offers in rhyme hilarious profiles of neighborhood buddies, can be used to spark middle-grade children to write their own character sketches. Who are the unusual people in their neighborhoods? What roles do they play in neighborhood dramas?

Children, in small groups, could then create improvisations involving these characters and the ways they interact when they come together. They might be browsing through the treasures of a yard sale, buying drinks at a lemonade stand, or searching for a runaway pet pig.

A Radio Play. Middle-grade children, in small groups, could develop radio plays using narration, dialogue, and sound effects. One play might involve a humorous tour of the neighborhood, capturing its distinctive sounds and featuring a number of "on the block" interviews. Another play might be a mystery about a secretive family that moves into the corner house of a city or suburban street. Where are these people from, and why do they always keep their windows closed and their curtains drawn? What are the strange sounds that emanate from the top floor? What are those strange creatures that they keep as pets? What happens when two neighborhood kids decide to investigate?

An Author-Themed Neighborhood Carnival. Middle-grade or older children could put together a neighborhood carnival for others. A Dr. Seuss-themed carnival might involve visitors building turtle towers with Yertle, making whimsical bonnets and hats with The Cat in the Hat, taking hatching lessons with Horton, or designing ecologically sound tree houses with the Lorax. At a Maurice Sendak carnival, visitors could learn how to "care" with Pierre, attend Really Rosie's fashion show, join in a ruckus with Max and the Wild Things, sample some chicken soup with rice, or make pastries in the Night Kitchen. At a Willam Steig neighborhood carnival, visitors could make Amos and Boris friendship rings, attend the trial of the Real Thief, learn to sulk like Spinky, invent new potions with Gorky, search for the Amazing Bone, or take a harmonica lesson from Zeke Pippin.

The Neighborhood Story Trunk. What are the tales that are passed down in a neighborhood—rescue tales, courtship tales, tales of irony and suspense? In the tiny European town of Kosnov, the people might still be chuckling about the sign in Mendel's window (Phillips) and the gossip it inspired and the commotion that it caused. The neighborhood people in *Hope and Glory* might describe the day when a lone German parachutist came floating down from the sky and all the ways people reacted. The villagers in *Sugar Cane Alley* will never forget the Old Storyteller and his glorious tales about Africa. This man was the spiritual center of their island community, the historian and story keeper.

Neighborhood stories are like wonderful glue. They bond people together and help them remember how things used to be. These stories need to be told, retold, and somehow recorded. In a storytelling session, children could share tales about a dramatic incident or special event that happened in their neighborhood. These might be about a visiting coyote, a winning raffle ticket, a wicked stickball game, or a Chinese dragon kite. For each story told, the teller could create a prop tied to that story that would be kept in the neighborhood story trunk.

Resources

Books

Bartone, Lisa. *Peppe the Lamplighter.* Lothrop, 1993.

Bunting, Eve. *Smoky Night.* Harcourt, 1994.

Day, David. *The Walking Catfish.* Simon, 1992.

Dooley, Norah. *Everybody Cooks Rice.* Carolrhoda, 1991.

Feelings, Muriel. *Zamani Goes to Market.* Seabury, 1970.

Fox, Mem. *Wilfred Gordon McDonald Partridge.* Kane/Miller, 1985.

Greenfield, Eloise. *Night on Neighborhood Street.* Dial, 1991.

Guy, Rosa. *Billy the Great.* Delacorte, 1991.

Haskins, Francine. *I Remember "121."* Children's Book Press, 1991.

Heide, Florence. *The Day of Ahmed's Secret.* Lothrop, 1990.

Hooks, William. *Circle of Fire.* McElderry, 1982.

Isadora, Rachel. *Ben's Trumpet.* Greenwillow, 1979.

Keats, Ezra. *Apartment 3.* Macmillan, 1971.

Keats, Ezra. *Dreams.* Macmillan, 1974.

Keats, Ezra. *Pet Show.* Macmillan, 1972.

Keats, Ezra. *Regards to the Man in the Moon.* Four Winds, 1981.

Keats, Ezra. *The Snowy Day.* Viking, 1962,

Keats, Ezra. *The Trip.* Macmillan, 1972.

Komaiko, Leah. *My Perfect Neighborhood.* Harper, 1990.

Lee, Harper. *To Kill a Mockingbird.* Harper, 1960.

Lessac, Frane. *Caribbean Canvas.* Boyds Mills, 1994.

Lewin, Hugh. *Jafta.* Carolrhoda, 1983.

Lewin, Hugh. *Jafta, the Homecoming.* Knopf, 1992.

Lewin, Hugh. *Jafta's Father.* Carolrhoda, 1983.

Lewis, Claudia. *Long Ago in Oregon.* Harper, 1987.

Phillips, Mildred. *The Sign in Mendel's Window.* Macmillan, 1983.

Polacco, Patricia. *Just Plain Fancy.* Bantam, 1990.

Prelutsky, Jack. *Rolling Harvey Down the Hill.* Greenwillow, 1980.

Provenson, Alice. *Shaker Lane.* Viking, 1987.

Raskin, Ellen. *Nothing Ever Happens on My Block.* Atheneum, 1966.

Ringgold, Faith. *Tar Beach.* Crown, 1991.

Robinson, Aminah. *A Street Called Home.* Harcourt, 1997.

Rylant, Cynthia. *An Angel for Solomon Singer.* Orchard, 1992.

Schick, Eleanor. *One Summer Night.* Greenwillow, 1977.

Schroeder, Alan. *Ragtime Tuppie.* Little, 1989.

Sendak, Maurice. *Chicken Soup with Rice.* HarperCollins.

Sendak, Maurice. *Pierre: A Cautionary Tale.* Harper, 1962.

Sendak, Maurice. *Where the Wild Things Are.* Harper, 1948.

Seuss, Dr. *The Cat in the Hat.* Random, 1957.

Seuss, Dr. *Horton Hatches a Who!* Random, 1954.

Seuss, Dr. *The Lorax.* Random, 1971.

Seuss, Dr. *Yertle the Turtle.* Random, 1958.

Singer, Marilyn. *Big Wheel.* Random, 1995.

Smalls-Hector, Irene. *Irene and the Big Fine Nickle.* Little, 1991.

Soto, Gary. *Neighborhood Odes.* Harcourt, 1992.

Spinelli, Jerry. *Maniac Magee.* Little, 1990.

Steig, William. *The Amazing Bone.* Farrar, 1976.

Steig, William. *Gorky Rises.* Farrar, 1980.

Steig, William. *The Real Thief.* Farrar, 1976.

Steig, William. *Spinky Sulks.* Farrar, 1988.

Steig, William. *Zeke Pippin.* HarperCollins, 1994.

Swope, Sam. *The Araboolies of Liberty Street.* Potter, 1989.

Van Allsburg, Chris. *The Widow's Broom.* Houghton, 1992.

Yezback, Steven. *Pumpkinseeds.* Bobbs-Merrill, 1969.

Yolen, Jane. *Letting Swift River Go.* Little, 1992.

Films, Videos, and DVDs

Hope and Glory, directed by John Boorman. Columbia, 1987. 112 minutes.

J.T. Carousel, 1969. 51 minutes.

The Neighbors. National Film Board of Canada, 1952. 9 minutes.

Really Rosie. Sheriss, 1976. 26 minutes.

Santiago's Ark. ABC, 1973. 47 minutes.

Sugar Cane Alley, directed by Euzhan Palcy. France, 1984. 103 minutes.

THEME 6:
The Movies ·· ●

When Amanda treats her great-uncle Max to a Saturday at The Palace of Stars (Lakin), she is once again awed by its gold and velvet texture. In this luxurious theater, her mind can dance and play and flicker about like the images on the giant screen. Everywhere there are pleasurable things to taste and see—nonpareils from the candy stand, stars on the ceiling, and the magical turns and glides of Fred Astaire. This world has a milieu of its own—a sort of fairy-tale splendor. It offers all those who enter an elegant shadow box, seductive marquees, uniformed ushers, chandeliers and balconies, ornate walls and red velvet curtains.

Even though these popcorn palaces have mostly been replaced by multiplex units in malls, the power of moviegoing can still transport children time and again. Through these celluloid journeys, they are able to cry and release emotions and to travel to lands of both menace and delight. Here, they encounter heroes and heroines and sometimes find characters like themselves with similar quirks and dreams.

The private aspect of moviegoing involves images filtered through a child's self-view and worldview that can arouse that child's yearnings. The collective part of moviegoing enables a child to be part of an audience and feel its electric charge, to yell in unison with others when the mighty King Kong rumbles across the screen, or to partake in a communal belly laugh when Shrek uses his earwax to make a candle.

Perhaps the most sweetly tinged moments occur in films about someone meeting a stranger and having his or her life affected forever. These are powerful moments—gentle, wistful, vivid—a rancher's son, Joey, offering his friendship to a loner called Shane; a lawyer's daughter, Scout, with directness and heart, reaching out to Boo Radley behind the front door.

An afternoon at the movies can inspire children to re-create scenes for the rest of the week, summoning up their own story lines and ideas. Joey, the movie lover in *The Pirates of Bedford Street* (Isadora) becomes immersed in a buccaneering epic about Captain Redbeard and continues the adventure with chalk in hand on his concrete stoop, creating a pirate universe.

The title character in *Starring Sally J. Freedman as Herself* (Blume) is very much cinema's child whether casting her imagined screenplays or roleplaying with Margaret O'Brien paper dolls. As a Jewish girl growing up in the late 1940s, she incorporates her hopes and anxieties into each new scenario, with the character of Adolf Hitler sometimes assuming a villainous role. This kind of pretending gives her a sense of order and control in a suddenly rocky and precarious world.

A third child obsessed with movies is Warren Otis, the 8-year-old dreamer in Betsy Byars's *The Two-thousand Pound Goldfish*. To Warren, the outside world is perpetually gray and unsettling, and the theater is his Technicolor refuge. Conjuring up film scripts is a way for him to deal with the pain of not knowing if he will ever see his mother. Warren's fertile and ingenious mind works like an editing machine, always framing and cutting scenes. As he develops the saga of Bubbles, a giant goldfish besieged by calamities, he is able to articulate and work through many of his own feelings.

Either one of two picture books could be used to launch an exploration of this theme. *On the Way to the Movies* (Herman) conveys the banter of two brothers heading to see a monster flick at the local theater. The patient, reassuring Simon is tested by his younger brother Freddie, who falls off a curb, scrapes his knee, and demands ice cream from the Dairy Queen. But while the two are waiting in line, detailed descriptions about "real" vampires with fangs create a twist in the tale and a surprising reversal in their feelings and roles.

A Perfect Day for the Movies (Chatalbash) sets up a dream device, which transports its heroine, Nancy, into the heart of the silver screen, where she engages in comic mayhem with the Three Stooges and tackles a mystery with Sherlock Holmes. What gives her the power to enter the screen, and who are those two strange cats hiding in her pockets? This book offers an intriguing concept and provocative visual style. Obviously, the author has a deep affection for classic films, providing many clever touches and references. Both of these books can elicit strong personal responses from children on their range of moviegoing experiences.

Developing a Film Program

Today, children as moviegoers are more sophisticated, more aware of process and technique. They can now rent and own DVDs and develop their own film libraries. They might even be makers of films and videos themselves. Also, the movies have changed as well. They are more global and represent more cultures. Minority children do not have to cringe every time their group is portrayed on screen, for stereotypes have begun to diminish, and characters are presented with more honesty and depth.

So many children are passionate about movies. They are always talking about this scene or that scene or how filmmakers achieved a certain effect. There is even pressure to keep up with the movies simply to know what others are talking about. Children may bond while discussing choice moments. They love to relive scenes word by word, gesture by gesture, recapturing each nuance, pause, and inflection.

A film program could introduce children to an eclectic sampling of films that they ordinarily would not be exposed to—films that include all genres, ranging from Bela Lugosi's *Dracula* to Charlie Chaplin's exquisitely choreographed *The Circus*. *A Chairy Tale* and *The Neighbors*, two short films produced by the National Film Board of Canada, can spark intense discussions among older children about the theme of "conflict."

Animated films to share with younger children are the beguiling *Moonbird* by the Hubleys, the whimsical *Dot and the Line*, and the haunting version of Raymond Briggs's *The Snowman*. *The Fur Coat Club* and *The Silver Whistle* are two live-action films that offer resourceful female protagonists.

Two international films focus on the day-to-day wishes and worries of children. *Le Poulet* is a humorous French film about one boy's efforts to prevent his pet chicken from becoming the family meal. Another pet at risk is *The Golden Fish*, the carnival prize of a young Chinese boy that just might become prey for a wandering alley cat. This film has a tense and startling climax.

Full-length films such as *Sounder* (Ritt) and *Where the Lilies Bloom* (Graham) can stimulate children to think about how literary works are translated to the screen. Do the core and spirit of a particular book remain intact? Other films to consider for viewing are the Weston Woods's adaptations of picture books and the wonderfully rendered folktales developed by Rabbit Ears Productions.

Sparking Film Discussions

Films can tap into feelings that children carry with them, and discussions based on these films can be lively and cathartic. In a safe and trusting environment, a feeling of mutual support may take place in which children realize that others may experience similar emotions. All children have yearnings and dreams, worries and concerns. All children have suffered through little indignities and, sometimes, big humiliations.

The young adolescents in the films *Big* (Marshall) and *King of the Hill* (Soderberg) must each endure an awkward, painful, diminishing moment, when their efforts to make a good impression dissolve in a wink and a flash. In these situations, time is the enemy, and the moment itself can seem prolonged and eternal.

In *Big*, Josh Baskin, despite his daring stance, is denied riding the killer attraction in an amusement park because he is not tall enough. Even worse, his rejection is witnessed by the older girl of his dreams, which makes this a salt-in-the-wounds, Class A double indignity.

The hero in the second film, Aaron Kurlander, is an inventive 12-year-old living in Depression-era St. Louis in one of the seedier hotels. He takes great pains to conceal his poverty and manufactures grand lies about knowing Charles Lindbergh and about his parents' identities and whereabouts.

When, at the graduation party, he overhears classmates mocking his ill-fitting clothes and describing him as a "charity case," Aaron feels trapped and exposed. His tall tales had not fooled anyone.

Both of these characters experience a sense of defeat and despair. How will they ever save face? How will they rebound after such blows to the spirit and heart?

What other little indignities might children have had to deal with, and how are they often tied to their vulnerabilities? Most likely, each child will have his or her catalog of deflating moments, of being shot down and ridiculed and made to feel small by bullies and unthinking adults. Who was in the pigeons' reading group and not the eagles, and who was always the last one picked for the softball game?

Some films address a child's yearnings and how they affect the choices that the child makes—offering clues on how that child operates in the world and interprets the events of his or her life.

The cherub-faced midwesterner Ralphie, in the film *A Christmas Story*, has an epiphany of a moment when he peers into the Christmas window of Higbee's grandly decorated department store. With his face pressed hard against the glass and so many toys to capture the eye, he spots it, his heart leaps, and there is no turning back.

It is this toy that he will think about, and dream about, and wish for in both his waking and sleeping hours. It will spark his imagination and inspire him to be extra phony and to bribe, and trick, and scheme. Young Ralphie just cannot help himself. He is so taken by the "Holy Grail of Christmas gifts"—the Red Ryder 200-shot, range model air rifle, the shiniest and most deluxe of BB guns.

How will his parents share his excitement when there are clearly safety issues? How can he drop a few hints without overplaying his hand?

When Ralphie, at school, is asked to write a theme about "What I Want for Christmas," he is sure this could be his breakthrough, his chance to make his plea and build his case. A glowing response from his teacher, Miss Shields, could shine a little light on his ambivalent parents and influence their big decision on how to reward him.

A very thoughtful Ralphie goes the extra mile by investing all his energy and skills. He has never felt so satisfied as when he completes his first serious piece of writing. He imagines Miss Shields, dancing with delight, using a word like "eloquent" or "extraordinary" to describe his style and content.

But when the themes are returned, Ralphie comes crashing to earth. The C+ on the top of the page shocks and dismays him, and the "P.S. You'll shoot your eye out" rubs more salt in his freshly stinging wounds.

What a crusher! What a jarring, heartbreaking moment! Maybe he had overestimated his literary gifts. Maybe he was not persuasive enough. Maybe his Christmas present to her, a well-stocked fruit basket, was more than a little transparent. Ralphie knows he must be resilient. He will never give up. He will just have to change his strategies.

Another child with deep yearnings is Pai, the heroine in *Whale Rider*. She is a natural leader—feisty, courageous, and very proud of her Maori ancestors. She is attuned to all aspects of her culture, both past and present. She wants to learn everything about being chief, for she feels that this is her rightful role. Already she knows the songs and chants by heart.

Her grandfather, the current chief, refuses to see that this is Pai's destiny. Even though he is wise in many ways, he cannot accept the idea of a female in this position. Still, he worries about his people not having a leader in the future to inspire them, and often he is profoundly sad.

The conflict between Pai and her grandfather is strong and intense, yet Pai tries to remain respectful even when he is extremely rejecting. When she is assertive, he becomes angry. When she expresses her yearnings, he refuses to listen. Constantly they are at odds.

But Pai is determined to achieve her dream, despite any doubts, frustrations, or setbacks. She listens to her strong inner voice, and this is what guides and sustains her.

A third child, Jose in *Sugar Cane Alley*, lives in the tropical island of Martinique in the 1930s and yearns to know about the larger world, especially his African roots. He is an 11-year-old who loves language and history and can be amazingly articulate.

Jose's pipe-smoking grandmother toils hard all day in the sugarcane fields. It is hot and uncomfortable and much of the time unbearable. What keeps her going is her dream. She is determined that Jose will have the finest education and escape a life of poverty. She sees how gifted he is, and that is why she pushes him so hard.

Sometimes Jose gets caught up in mischief with the children of the village, especially when all the grown-ups are working. Once someone causes a fire, and another time others invite themselves into Jose's shack, despite his resistance, and accidentally break his grandmother's special dish. You can see how bad he feels because he has let her down and acted in an irresponsible way. He even tries to lie, and this makes matters worse.

Being so curious about everything, Jose is a boy who makes friends with people of all ages. The old, eloquent storyteller inspires him with tales of Africa and what used to be, and the young, roguish boat driver explains to him about romantic things, and, in turn, Jose teaches him how to read.

Often, Jose demonstrates his courage and willfulness. He is always true to himself, despite the consequences. When the teacher accuses him of plagiarizing because his writing is so poetic and sophisticated, Jose refuses to back down and waits for an apology.

When Jose receives a scholarship to attend a high school in the city, their dream is realized, but this puts extra pressure on his grandmother. Where will they live, and how can she pay for the additional expenses?

A film like *The Red Balloon* can stimulate younger children to share stories about their favorite toy or possession and how they would feel if it were to get broken or lost.

What a lucky day for Pascal, an only child, when he finds a big, red balloon tied to a lamppost while walking to school. That first morning, he leaves his new treasure with the school janitor. At the end of the day, he makes the long walk home since balloons are not allowed on city buses.

When he explains why he was late to his worried mother, she is not sympathetic. In fact, she opens the window and lets the balloon fly away. Pascal, of course, is extremely sad. But then a magical thing occurs. Pascal sees the balloon hovering outside his window. It seems to actually have a will of its own. The delighted boy lets the balloon inside and hides it in his room.

This is a friendship story—a friendship that is both playful and protective. The two become companions who like to trick each other and go exploring. They even have a sweet, flirtatious encounter with a young girl and her blue balloon. Pascal, for once in his life, is not so lonely.

Because the balloon is mischievous and does not always obey, Pascal finds himself in some troubling situations. When the balloon follows Pascal into the classroom, there is a great commotion, with the principal getting involved and a punished Pascal getting locked in his office. When the balloon follows Pascal and his mother into church, the whole congregation becomes distracted, and the church guard has to escort Pascal and his embarrassed mother outside.

But the real problems begin when a gang of rowdy neighborhood boys spots the balloon. They are determined to either possess it or destroy it, and the most exciting scenes involve Pascal and his balloon running through the streets and alleys of Paris trying to escape from them.

The Red Balloon provides a real sense of a Parisian neighborhood in the 1950s. This is a quiet film, very visual, and there is hardly any dialogue. The ending is like a small miracle and should enchant children, taking their breath away. They may want to discuss how these last scenes were created.

Evaluating Films

Children as young as 9 or 10 years could be encouraged to develop their own set of criteria for evaluating films. They should be able to describe the story line and elaborate on its conflict. How is the plot resolved, and does the resolution seem plausible?

In analyzing the main characters, children should consider if they are complex or superficial. What motivates their actions? Do the filmmakers create a vivid sense of place? Is the film fresh and original? Does it take risks or simply adhere to a formula? What is the film's point of view? Is the film authentic in its portrayal of a group? Does it capture the language, concerns, and humor of the group? Is the film in any way stereotypical?

Children could explore which scenes are the most and least effective. They could assess the strengths and weaknesses of a film in terms of directing, acting, pacing, editing, scoring, cinematography, art direction, costume design, and special effects. How might a film be challenging, affecting, or provocative?

Concluding Thoughts

Movies are a romantic medium, extending boundaries and nourishing imaginations. Through careful viewing and discussion, they may foster in children feelings of empathy. They may ease children's anxieties during disconnected times when they present characters who are also struggling to survive.

Images pop up of two runaway Irish brothers in *Into the West* seeking sanctuary in an empty movie house with their magical white horse. Images come to mind of a troubled Ralph in *Lord of the Flies* calling others with his conch, wanting to restore reason and order, but achingly knowing he has lost his power and command. As illustrated here, the medium of film can be an amazing tool, encouraging children to see the complexity of people, to take a stand, and sometimes even to challenge their own assumptions.

Creative Excursions

The Flipbook Project. Younger children could examine some flipbooks and then actually learn how to make them. Next, they could develop simple story lines before beginning their project. These books might have titles such as The Butterfly's Journey, Where's My Balloon? or The Adventures of a Kite.

The Artists' Guild. Middle-grade or older children could make reel-to-reel shoe-box panoramas; research and demonstrate the use of movie makeup; develop a portrait galley of old-time comedy stars; design posters of their imagined screenplays or of favorite chapter books that have yet to be adapted into films; build a miniature movie palace in a box; or develop a storyboard for an animated film idea. *Alexander and the Car with a Missing Headlight,* a delightful video with an improvised quality, could inspire children to make a short animated film in which they create the watercolor backgrounds, the characters, the voices of the characters, and the sound effects.

The Writers' Guild. Middle-grade or older children, working in pairs or in small groups, could develop original scenarios and screenplays—an ecological story about the last tiger on earth, a comedy that takes place in a joke factory, a mystery that occurs on a baseball field, or a science fiction spoof called The Gerbil That Wrecked the Bronx. They might simply be given a title as a starting point to stimulate their thinking (Imagination Alley, Lunchbox Blues, The Boy with Cheese in His Head, The First Laugh, The Autograph Hound, or Spirit on a One-Night Stand). When the screenplays are complete, children could have a special reading.

The Actors' Guild.   Middle-grade or older children could create improvisations about a movie extra who tries to be a part of each scene, two adventurers who sneak into an empty movie set at night; famous movie pairs, as children, meeting each other for the first time (Sherlock Holmes and Moriarity, Fred and Ginger, the good-natured Stan and the grumpy Oliver); misguided characters involved in disastrous auditions (Popeye trying out for the role of Hamlet); a blabbering moviegoer who disrupts the showing of a serious art film, complaining when there are no cartoons and carrying on when he finds the letter "V" on one of his "M and M's." Some children could create a pantomime play in the spirit of the old silent films and melodramas. Their play might have title and text cards and some kind of musical accompaniment, and fresh popcorn could be served as a snack.

Runaway Blues.   *The Little Fugitive,* with its striking black-and-white images, could introduce children to one of the earliest independent films. It was shot on location with a very low budget, using nonprofessional actors. There is hardly any dialogue.

In the film, a mean trick perpetuated by his big brother Lenny causes Joey, a 7-year-old, to run away to Coney Island on a hot summer's day. Joey wrongly thinks he has killed Lenny with a toy gun, so heads off to this huge amusement park, taking the subway all by himself.

In such a loud, gyrating world, Joey can immerse himself in a whirl of activities. This way he does not have to think about Lenny or his mom or his troubling predicament. He can meander around, absorbing all the seductive images and smells. He can try out a few games and maybe win a few prizes.

During his first few hours, Joey feasts on hot dogs, fries, and watermelon. He loves riding both the real ponies and the carved beauties of the carousel. With his cowboy hat and rugged spirit, Joey proves he can be independent and resourceful. He learns to navigate through the crowds, and rarely does he seem overwhelmed. After he runs out of money, he scavenges for bottles, turning them in for coins.

That night, he sleeps safely under the boardwalk. And when he wakes up, for a short period, he has this entire universe to himself. Sitting up in the lifeguard station, Joey can appreciate the crashing of the waves and the vastness of the sea. It is all so peaceful now—no babies crying, no vendors calling out, no people screaming wildly on the Cyclone.

But eventually, Joey needs to connect with someone. He cannot escape forever, and he is keeping so many feelings inside. What will he do when his clothes get too dirty, and when will he start missing his mom?

The Little Fugitive is an amazing survival tale that captures New York tenement life in the 1950s and is a wonderful introduction to one of the world's most famous amusement parks. Children will root for and identify with this plucky kid and wonder how they would fare if they found themselves in his situation. The film should provoke discussion about misunderstandings, problems with siblings, and things that upset children enough that they would consider running away from home.

Mystery Movie Game.   Older children can challenge each other to identify a "mystery movie" by naming an important prop from the film. These might include a skateboard, umbrella, wilting rose, or bag of Reese's Pieces. They might also want to give a line of dialogue as a clue.

"Feed me!"

"Auntie Em! Auntie Em!"

"May the force be with you!"

"Do you know the Muffin Man?"

Investigative Journeys.   Older children could formulate research questions related to filmmaking and film history and present their findings in an exciting fashion.

Who created the first movies? What kind of equipment did they use? What were the contributions of Thomas Edison and the Lumiere brothers? Who were the stars of early comedies? How did various genres evolve—westerns, musicals, horror, and science fiction films? What problems occurred during the transition between silent films and talkies? Why has the powerful icon King Kong endured for so many years? Why did 3-D films seem to fade after the 1950s?

How are special effects created? What are the various animation techniques (clay, cel drawings, pixillation, puppetry, computer graphics)? How is filmmaking a collaborative process? What is the division of labor? What are the problems inherent in filming on location? How dangerous is the work of stunt people? Are films always shot in sequence? How painstaking is the editing process? What do actors do between takes? How do art directors and costume designers create other times and worlds?

How did the old studio system operate in Hollywood? What are independent films, and how are they financed? How has the film industry encouraged or impeded women and minority filmmakers? What are the experiences of child actors? What pressures are put on them? How do they keep up with their school work?

Resources

Books

Anderson, Yvonne. *Make Your Own Animated Movies and Videotapes.* Little, 1991.

Blume, Judy. *Starring Sally J. Freedman as Herself.* Bradbury, 1977.

Byars, Betsy. *The Two-thousand Pound Goldfish.* Harper, 1982.

Chatalbash, Ron. *A Perfect Day for the Movies.* Godine, 1983.

Cherrell, Gwen. *How Movies Are Made.* Facts on File, 1989.

Cohen, Daniel. *Masters of Horror.* Clarion, 1984.

Gibbons, Gail. *Lights! Camera! Action!* Crowell, 1985.

Hargrove, Jim. *Steven Spielberg: Amazing Filmmaker.* Children's Book Press, 1987.

Herman, Charlotte. *On the Way to the Movies.* Dutton, 1980.

Hunter, Nigel. *The Movies.* Raintree, 1990.

Isadora, Rachel. *The Pirates of Bedford Street.* Greenwillow, 1980.

Lakin, Patricia. *The Palace of Stars.* Tambourine, 1993.

Lobel, Arnold. *Martha the Movie Mouse.* Harper, 1993.

Snyder, Carol. *Ike and Mama and the Once-in-a-Lifetime Movie.* Coward, 1981.

Films, Videos, and DVDs

Alexander and the Car with a Missing Headlight. Weston Woods, 1966. 14 minutes.

Animation Pie. Wright, 1975. 15 minutes.

Arrow to the Sun. Texture, 1973. 12 minutes.

Big, directed by Penny Marshall. Fox, 1994. 104 minutes.

A Chairy Tale. National Film board of Canada, 1957. 10 minutes.

The Chicken (Le Poulet). Contemporary, 1965. 10 minutes.

A Christmas Story, directed by Bob Clark. Warner, 1983. 98 minutes.

Cinema Paradiso, directed by Giuseppe Tornatore, Italy, 1990. 123 minutes.

The Circus, directed by Charlie Chaplin. United Artists, 1928. 72 minutes.

Cooley High, directed by Michael Schultz. American International, 1975. 107 minutes.

The Dot and the Line. Film, 1965. 9 minutes.

Dracula, directed by Tod Browning. Universal, 1931. 84 minutes.

The Fur Coat Club. Learning Corporation, 1973. 19 minutes.

The Golden Fish. Columbia, 1962. 20 minutes.

Hope and Glory, directed by John Boorman. Columbia, 1987. 112 minutes.

Into the West, directed by Mike Newell. Touchstone, 1993. 97 minutes.

J.T. Carousel, 1969. 51 minutes.

King of the Hill, directed by Steven Soderberg.

The Little Fugitive, directed by Ray Ashley. Burstyn, 1953. 75 minutes.

Lord of the Flies, directed by Peter Brook. England, 1963. 90 minutes.

Madeline. UPA, 1952. 7 minutes.

Moonbird. Images, 1959. 10 minutes.

The Neighbors. National Film board of Canada, 1952. 9 minutes.

People Soup. Learning Corporation, 1969. 13 minutes.

Red Ball Express. Perspective, 1976. 3 minutes.

The Red Balloon. Macmillan, 1959. 34 minutes.

Santiago's Ark. Carousel, 1973. 47 minutes.

The Silver Whistle. FilmFair, 1981. 17 minutes.

Skater Dater. Pyramid, 1965. 18 minutes.

The Snowman, directed by Dianne Jackson. Columbia, 1982. 23 minutes.

Sounder, directed by Martin Ritt. Radnitz, 1972.

Sugar Cane Alley, directed by Euzhan Palcy. France, 1983. 103 minutes.

To Kill a Mockingbird, directed by Robert Mulligan. Universal, 1962. 129 minutes.

Whale Rider, directed by Niki Caro. Newmarket, 2003. 105 minutes.

Where the Lilies Bloom, directed by William Graham. United Artists, 1974. 97 minutes.

THEME 7:
When Trouble Comes ⋯⋯⋯⋯⋯⋯⋯⋯⋯⋯⋯⋯⋯⋯⋯⋯⋯ ●

In a popular tale from *The Knee-High Man* (Lester), the mean-spirited Mr. Rabbit cannot believe his ears when the naive Mr. Bear explains that he does not know what the word "trouble" means. For some reason, this exasperates Mr. Rabbit, who decides to spell it out for him, to demonstrate what "trouble" is, in a way that Mr. Bear will never forget.

He tells the eager Mr. Bear to simply go to sleep in the meadow, and soon the meaning will become quite clear. When Mr. Bear wakes up, he smells smoke all around and begins to panic.

Everywhere the grass is on fire, and so Mr. Bear hightails it to safety, crying "Trouble! Trouble!" In the distance, the smug Mr. Rabbit yells back, "Now you know, Mr. Bear. You know what trouble is." One cruel trick played and one lesson learned. Of course, the scorched and livid Mr. Bear will never trust Mr. Rabbit again.

When Professor Harold Hill, the razzle-dazzle con artist in the film *The Music Man,* warns the parents of River City that trouble might be brewing right under their noses, he is able to rile them up and create a terrific uproar. He identifies swearing trouble, dime-novel trouble, and pool-hall trouble. Within minutes, the parents are alarmed and aghast. What is happening with their children?

When the young hero in *The Sandlot* takes his stepfather's Babe Ruth autographed ball to use in a neighborhood game, that is when trouble comes. When Babe, the wanting-to-be-helpful pig, becomes an accomplice in the duck's scheme to steal the farmer's alarm clock, that is when Mr. Trouble snarls with delight.

"Trouble" is indeed a loaded word. Just the mention of it can start a child's pulse racing, produce anxiety, or cause someone's eyes to well with tears. For children, often the most impacting moments in books and films involve a character on the threshold of getting into trouble and moving close to the precarious edge. Children enter into these scenes fully, for they identify with a character's feelings of apprehension and discomfort.

Children could define "trouble" in their own terms and reflect on their own experiences. They might want to compile a "trouble list" of the kinds of situations that could put them in the "doghouse" or lead them to the gallows. How would any of these situations rate on the trouble scale? How would one measure their weight and severity? What might be a "1" and what might be a "10"?

A "Trouble" List

Disobeying a parent.

Breaking a rule.

Breaking a neighbor's window.

Losing something valuable.

Forgetting to watch a pet or a younger sibling.

Telling a lie.

Getting a bad report card.

Getting sent to the principal's office.

Children could also discuss the consequences of their acts and the range of punishments that might result. When confronted by an angry grown-up or peer, do they accept responsibility or hedge and look for a way out? How do they deal with the fallout or aftermath when there are no spin doctors around to do damage control? How can they save face? Do they apologize, deny, make up excuses, or try to shift the blame?

What are the ways that children get punished, and do these punishments fit their crimes? Some children are sent to "time out" or told they cannot play outside. Some may lose their allowances or their television, computer, or phone privileges. Others may be spanked, grounded, or denied their favorite desserts.

Getting into trouble is a common occurrence when children go out into the world. When Jimmy, in *The Day Jimmy's Boa Ate the Wash* (Noble), brings his pet snake on a class field trip to a farm, havoc ensues as chickens go berserk, pigs raid the children's lunches, and the children themselves engage in corn and egg fights. This story humorously illustrates how owning a pet can lead to a calamity or two.

The heroine in *The Lost Umbrella of Kim Chu* (Estes) is upset when, after an outing to the library, she sees that her father's prized umbrella has been taken. She experiences a moment of dread as she anticipates how she might be punished and feels profound pain. She knows she has let her father down and violated his trust in her by taking the umbrella without permission.

Harriet the Spy (Fitzhugh) feels exposed, frantic, and paranoid when she sees her classmates reading her secret notebook and all its revelations, asides, and on-target observations. Her words are hurting and cut to the quick. She describes, for example, her friend Sport as "worrying all the time and fussing over his father . . . like a little old woman." Other descriptions are equally devastating. What was private is now public, and she is about to alienate all those in her school world.

Sometimes children step into trouble when they collide with a bully or regular "rough, tough" older guys. Herbie's Troubles (Chapman) begin when Jimmy John enters his world at school destroying his sand tunnel, smashing his granola bar, and keeping him hostage in the bathroom stall. How does a 6-year-old deal with having his own private nemesis?

Ada Potato (Caseley) encounters trouble when she is taunted by older kids as she walks through the "dark and smelly" tunnel under the railroad tracks. Sometimes they try to take her violin, but Ada gets the upper hand when she recruits her musician friends and resolves her dilemma with imagination and verve.

Little Eight John (Wahl) is constantly challenging his mother's advice and disobeying her in ways sneaky and deliberate. He seems to have a prickly, insolent nature. When he ignores family superstitions—sleeping with his head at the foot of the bed and kicking toad frogs, trouble is just waiting in the wings.

Trouble is not restricted to one gender. *Queenie Peavy* (Burch), always at a stone's throw from being expelled, is unfazed by her trips to the principal's office and considers them badges of honor. Her catalog of transgressions includes cursing, chewing tobacco, swearing, fighting, and throwing rocks in the boiler room.

Troubadours of trouble also exist in the realm of folktales and myths. Iktomi, the Dakota Indian trickster in *Iktomi and the Buzzard* (Goble), exploits the goodwill of Buzzard with fake tears to get a ride across the river and then has the nerve to mock him during the flight. This is why Iktomi has been dropped inside a tree hollow and is now feeling trapped and isolated.

In the Italian tale *Strega Nona* (DePaola), Big Anthony is warned by his employer, the town's Grandma Witch, not to touch the magic pasta pot while she is away on a visit. Unfortunately, Big Anthony cannot resist this chance to try out the special words he has heard her use, and soon the overflowing pasta is flooding the entire town. In this case, the punishment is perfect, and Big Anthony may never want to taste a strand of pasta again.

Loki and Pan, the two classic troublemakers of Norse and Greek mythology, are masters of mischief, often provoking others and sparking conflicts through their meddling. In many of these tales, they are catalysts, stirring things up and guaranteeing a bit of chaos.

This is why angry Thor in *Stolen Thunder* (Climo) accuses Loki of stealing his hammer from under his bed. Who else would instigate such a prank? Is it possible that Loki is innocent this time?

In *Tales of Pan* (Gerstein), the pipe-playing title character is credited with inventing panic. When an ant with a cold disturbs his sleep, Pan makes such a discordant sound that it reverberates all through Arcadia, causing animals to run amok and nymphs to get "tangled in trees."

Acts of Bravado

Sometimes children speak in "bravado" or "dare language"—a sort of inflated big talk with puffed-up posturing. They speak it mostly when they are showing off or saving face, or when they are testing limits or defying those in authority.

Much of "dare language" is developmental, healthy, and even humorous. It may be used to demonstrate one's prowess or to secure one's position in a group. In dodge ball, players speak it when they yell, "Get me!" "Hit me!" In baseball, the catcher may use it to intimidate or distract the batter.

In stories, Pierre speaks it repeatedly when he proclaims, "I don't care!" Oliver Twist is forced to speak it, after losing the draw, when he confronts Mr. Bumble with "Please, Sir, I want some more." Huck Finn, a master bluffer and tall-tale spinner, speaks and lives "dare" on a minute-to-minute, hour-to-hour basis. This gift is his resource and often his only survival tool.

Naturally, acts of bravado can lead to all kinds of trouble. Sometimes they result when challenges escalate and someone impulsively ups the ante, "I dare you, and then I double dare you." Such is the case in *How to Eat Fried Worms* (Rockwell) when Billy, the main character, accepts a bet to eat fifteen worms in fifteen days. In this outrageous tale, the young hero is spurred on by his dream of buying a fifty-dollar mini-bike. How does he prepare for worm number one? What condiments can make a night crawler seem more appetizing—barbecue sauce, mustard, or sour cream?

Some acts of bravado are secret and private—a child testing something out or trying to prove something by riding the wildest horse or skateboarding down the sharpest curve. But even these acts can have consequences and may seem foolish or dangerous on reflection.

Mouse, the protagonist in Betsy Byars's *The Eighteenth Emergency*, has a humorous slant on life and is always labeling the things in his world with tiny letters and arrows. It is this habit that gets him into serious trouble. When he writes the name Marv Hammerman on an anthropology chart with an arrow pointing to the Neanderthal Man, the moment is witnessed by the legendary bully himself. This private, impulsive, irresistible act will soon be part of school history, for Hammerman has vowed his revenge.

To pull off a dare can be releasing and exhilarating. Some dares lead children to places forbidden. Almost any neighborhood has a taboo place—a haunted locale where nightmares fester. Each of these places has an aura, a history, a power of its own. They may have unusual smells, unsettling sounds, or mysterious lights. Legends grow and are passed down. Superstitions spread. Children may feel compelled to approach or to even enter these ominous worlds, so they can wrestle with and confront their fears.

In *Maniac Magee* (Spinelli), the place to avoid is the Finsterwalds at 803 Oriole Street, for those who get too close may be cursed with the finsterwallies—"a violent trembling of the body, especially in the extremities."

In *To Kill a Mockingbird* (Lee), it is Boo Radley's home, "droopy and sick," that has such a hold on Jem and Scout Finch and their summer friend Dill. Is the evil contained inside, or could it spill out into the night? Why would just eating pecans from the Radley trees probably kill a person? And will Jem, "who has never declined a bet," take leave of his senses and sneak past the Radley gate and actually touch Boo Radley's house?

What happens when children play on the edge, flirting with danger and then scurrying back? Will they cross the line? Will they lose control? Will their actions lead them to a point of no return? What happens when there are unclear boundaries? Will someone in the group be a tempering force, a voice for reason and safety?

The seven children in Donald Crews's *Shortcut*, for a brief stretch of time, enjoy the false security of being safe in a group. Feeling carefree and omnipotent, they disobey the grown-ups and take the shortcut, walking the tracks, scuffling, and singing with voices in high volume.

Time seems suspended as they are caught up in the spirit of the dare. But soon a new sound invades, and a whistle blows louder and louder. All at once they are genuinely scared and truly at risk. When they jump off the track, they can feel the immense power of the giant train passing. These are harrowing moments. Afterward, on the safe path home, they share a sense of relief and shame and a long extended silence.

The setup of an approaching train and children on the threshold of panicking is also used in the film *Stand by Me*. This whole film is a dare brought to life and centers on four 12-year-old boys who embark on a two-day journey to find the dead body of a missing boy, after first lying to their parents.

On this odyssey, they sustain a high level of bravado—teasing, tussling, exchanging masterful insults and creative curses, and especially enjoying their after-dinner "smoke" around an evening campfire. The most excitable of the four is Teddy Dechamp, short-fused and nervy, obsessed with the military and the Texas Rangers. The group puts up with him because Teddy has "guts" and a generous spirit. He is a daring and impulsive guy who likes to take chances, and the others often have to bail him out.

Tales of Redemption

When children believe they have done something wrong, they are not always sure how to make amends and turn things around. They may have let down a friend, been disloyal to a parent, or severely disappointed themselves. A wrongdoing may gnaw at them, affecting their study habits, appetites, even invading their dreams.

Because it is impossible to go back in time and erase certain deeds, they have to acknowledge their wrongdoing and take responsibility in order to redeem themselves. It is one thing to say, "I'm sorry," but what specific actions could they take that would be constructive and restorative?

Repairing the damage can help children to grow, to be honest and accountable. It can unburden them, freeing them of the heavy, troubling feelings that they carry inside. It might even help them to be reflective. What motivated them in the first place to commit such an act? Was it a lapse in judgment? Were they, at the time, simply oblivious?

> My father looked at the garden, trampled and ruined, and it was only then that he realized what he had done. (*The Summer My Father Was Ten*, Brisson)

In *The Summer My Father Was Ten* (Brisson), the narrator's father, a boy at the time, feels genuine remorse for the damage he causes when he instigates a tomato and pepper fight after a baseball is hit into a neighbor's garden. This was a spontaneous act, playful and thoughtless, but not calculated or malicious.

It begins innocently and then escalates. A group of boys get caught up in roughhousing. They love the messiness and juiciness of it all, the joy of dodging flying tomatoes, and the even greater joy of seeing them splatter and explode. Soon flowers and vegetables are uprooted, and the boys are covered with seeds, pulp, and red and green stains.

The destructiveness of their play does not set in until Mr. Bellavista, the owner of the garden, steps forward. The grim-faced man is hurt and shaken. "Why?" he asks. He does not need to say anything else.

This one word has an enormous and enduring power, haunting the boy all through the year, especially when he sees the man on the steps coming from or going to his third-floor apartment. The boy has really never thought much about Mr. Bellavista, let alone reached out to him. In fact, he and his friends had referred to him as "old spaghetti man" and made fun of his strong accent, solitary ways, and the fact that he always wears flannel shirts, even in the summer.

When April comes, the boy offers to help Mr. Bellavista plant a new garden, and the old man senses that he is committed and sincere. The boy becomes his apprentice, learning all about planting and weeding. He also learns the secret of making a fresh, tasty tomato sauce. The two begin to share some meals together, listening to different operas on the radio.

Both are enriched by their new friendship. The old man becomes less alone in the world and is able to share his legacy. The boy becomes the receiver of his knowledge and a lifelong gardener, who, like Mr. Bellavista, finds solace and delight working in the soil. Many years later, the boy, now a father, is able to share his passion with his son.

This lovely, emotional, and understated tale is really about healing and starting anew. It illustrates how one child, after making a big mistake, finds a way of doing the right thing. Through the risk that he takes, he is able to move forward, forgive himself, and help an old man to be more open and trusting.

Sometimes children and young adults cave in to peer pressure in their need to be accepted. They worry about their status and choose to conform and may be willing to surrender their values.

The act committed by a group of four boys in *The Boy Who Lost His Face* (Sachar) is a cruel, appalling, and calculated act. It is especially disturbing for it is intended to cause harm to an eccentric and vulnerable old woman.

During the incident that takes place in her yard, the boys mock and deride her. They call her nasty names and ruin her flowerbed. Besides stealing her walking cane (their original goal), they push her over in her rocking chair and pour lemonade on her face—the same lemonade she offered them in kindness. In doing this, they put her at risk. What if she were severely injured or traumatized?

In just a few short minutes, these boys have become vandals and perpetrators of evil. What is worse is that they seem to delight in being so vicious, except for David, the title character, who only flipped her the finger.

David, in his efforts to hold on to his best friend and enter the popular clique, has disgraced himself and disrespected an innocent woman. He, of the four, is capable of feeling compassion and empathy and imagines his baby sister, as an older person, being targeted and victimized by mean-spirited strangers. David knows he has crossed the line, and now he feels wounded and distressed. He has been a part of something ugly, but never once did he protest or try to dissuade the others.

What can he do now? Should he apologize, and if he does, would such a gesture seem pointless, or hollow, or false? How does he redeem himself and reclaim his integrity? Are certain acts, such as this one, so heinous that they are unforgivable?

Although the theme of Trouble has a playful, humorous dimension, it is also a theme that is powerful and provocative and can stimulate a number of intense discussions. For children, being or getting into trouble can cause them to feel diminished. Any day can be filled with troubling situations. What if they forget to lock the front door? What if they meet up with the school bully on the bus or playground? What if they lose someone's confidence or respect? What if they get caught cheating on a test? What if they are pressured by peers to misbehave, to cheat or steal or vandalize something? Discussions of these works can help children identify areas of stress and concern and different approaches to problem solving.

Creative Excursions

The Time-Out Players. Younger children, after listening to *The Thinking Place* (Joose), could create little dramas or puppet plays about an animal who has to go to "time out" for being naughty, ill-mannered, or disobedient. A young skunk might be punished for stinking up Mrs. Squirrel's birthday picnic. An owl might be in trouble for being too noisy when his mother is taking her all-day nap. A rabbit may find herself in a jam when she ignores farm etiquette and steals one carrot too many from the farmer's garden.

Old Man Trouble. Younger children, after listening to *Aunt Nancy and Old Man Trouble* (Root), might want to draw their own versions of this well-dressed villain or make up stories about his encounters with others who might live in Aunt Nancy's neighborhood. Will they be as shrewd as she is in finding clever means to outwit him?

Bully Trouble. Younger children, through discussion, could explore issues tied to dealing with bullies. To introduce this subject, the group leader could read aloud *Bootsie Barker Bites* (Bottner). In this tale, the heroine dreads whenever her mother's friend comes for a visit and brings her daughter Bootsie with her. The young hostess is expected to entertain Bootsie, but it never quite works out that way, for Bootsie is a mean-spirited girl, fiendish and gleefully cruel, a master of torment and torture. Under the guise of fantasy play, she likes to engage in hair pulling and trying out new wrestling holds. How can the story's gentle heroine put a stop to Bootsie Barker, and how does her imagination help her to triumph?

Making Things Right. Middle-grade children could read, examine, and explore books that deal with the theme of Redemption. How does a specific character make amends to right a wrong? Is the character's solution well conceived and effective? Is the wronged person open to working things out? In *The Hundred Dresses* (Estes), for example, does writing a friendly letter to Wanda Petronski even begin to make up for the ugly ways Peggy and Maddie have treated her? Children might wish to share some of their own sorrows and regrets about how they acted in different situations.

Troublesome Traits. Middle-grade children could identify certain negative personality traits, including their own. How might having such a trait create problems for that person or lead that person into troublesome situations? How can being too noisy, too lazy, too messy, too bossy, or too stubborn cause others to react with anger or annoyance? In small groups, children could develop humorous skits to emphasize these traits. One group, for example, might bring to life Stubborn School where Pierre teaches different ways of saying, "I don't care!" and Mildred S. Mule demonstrates how to balk, stay in one position, and never budge an inch.

The Do-It-Yourself Girl. Middle-grade children could develop an improvised play about an ill-mannered and sassy girl named Rowena living during fairy-tale times. Why is she so troublesome to others, and what happens when she wanders about the countryside searching for ripe, juicy blueberries to fill up her bucket? On her quest, whom does she encounter? Some possibilities:

- A panicky Jack, climbing quickly down the beanstalk, who begs her to run and get him an axe. Rowena snaps back, "Don't be lazy. Do it yourself!"
- A lost Hansel and Gretel who ask her to help them make a trail of bread crumbs. Rowena replies, "I don't care much for bread. I like muffins, so do it yourself!"
- A frustrated pig who asks for help in building a house of straw. Rowena snottily explains, "I'm no architect. Do it yourself!"
- An overworked Snow White who asks for some housekeeping help. Rowena answers, "Are you kidding? I'm allergic to dust. Do it yourself!"
- A depressed Prince who needs help in finding the girl who lost her glass slipper at the Ball. Rowena scowls, "So why wasn't I invited? Find her yourself!"

Suppose a wicked wolf chases Rowena up into a tree, and the rude Rowena experiences some genuinely scary moments. What if a wise wizard were to rescue her, reminding her how mean and thoughtless she was, and encouraging her to be more courteous? What happens the very next day when Geppeto asks her for help in building his puppet boy? How does Rowena respond? Has she learned an important lesson? Will she be polite and reach out, or will she simply revert to her old ways?

The Curse. Beware of these words! "Your Doppleganger will regurgitate on your soul." This fake, made-up curse, created on the spot by Mrs. Bayfield in *The Boy Who Lost His Face*, could be used to stimulate middle-grade children to make up stories centering on a curse. These tales could be both humorous and suspenseful.

Maps of Forbidden Places. Children are drawn to the forbidden places they read or hear about, especially the ones in their own neighborhood. They want to know who or what they might encounter in these worlds. To play with this idea, they could each create maps of their real or imagined forbidden places and then develop legends describing how these places came to be. Their forbidden place might take the form of an abandoned theater, a boxcar in a railroad yard, or a giant sandpit or crater. Why do these places both attract and repel? Who, if anyone, resides there—a guardian or caretaker, a malevolent spirit or spiteful gnome? Are there secret ways of entering these settings without being seen? These maps should be vivid and detailed, each with a strong, disturbing power.

Impossible Guests.   Dr. Seuss's *The Cat in the Hat* and Edward Gorey's *The Doubtful Guest* are terrific examples of outrageous visitors who come to visit unannounced. One exits in the knick of time, but the other has no intention of leaving. Either book could be used to initiate this activity in which pairs of middle-grade children develop scenes that involve a gracious host and an extreme kind of guest. How do the two interact? Are there any dramatic sparks, and is there ever a time when the host or hostess starts feeling impatient and out of control? Such vignettes might be titled:

The Apologetic Guest.
The Ghostly Guest.
The Whining Guest.
The "Don't Mind Me" Guest.
The Giggling Guest.
The "Take Over" Guest.
The Gung Ho Guest.
The "I'll Tell Mama" Guest.
The Super Clean and Tidy Guest.

A Salute to Eddie Haskell.   Older children could view episodes of *Leave It to Beaver,* focusing on the character of Eddie Haskell, and discuss how this character is a genuine troublemaker. Why is he both obnoxious and endearing? They could then create roleplaying situations of Eddie tormenting little Beaver or of Eddie being extra phony in his chats with Wally and Beaver's mother, June.

Illustrating the Blues.   Older children, after listening to Simon and Garfunkel's "Bridge over Troubled Waters" and recordings of Alberta Hunter, Billie Holliday, and other blues artists, could design black-and-white posters or create paintings that convey the moods of these works, capturing their melancholy and sorrow.

Resources

Books

Adler, David A. *The Children of Chelm.* Bonim, 1979.
Bottner, Barbara. *Bootsie Barker Bites.* Putnam, 1992.
Brisson, Pat. *The Summer My Father Was Ten.* Boyds Mill, 1998.
Bunting, Eve. *Smoky Night.* Harcourt, 1994.
Burch, Robert. *Queenie Peavy.* Viking, 1966.
Byars, Betsy. *The 18th Emergency.* Viking, 1973.

Caseley, Judith. *Ada Potato*. Greenwillow, 1989.

Chapman, Carol. *Herbie's Troubles*. Dutton, 1981.

Climo, Shirley. *Stolen Thunder*. Clarion, 1994.

Crews, Donald. *Shortcut*. Greenwillow, 192.

DePaola, Tomie. *Strega Nona*. Prentice, 1985.

Estes, Eleanor. *The Hundred Dresses*. Harcourt, 1944.

Estes, Eleanor. *The Lost Umbrella of Kim Chu*. Atheneum, 1978.

Fitzhugh, Louise. *Harriet the Spy*. Harper, 1964.

Gerstein, Mordicai. *Tales of Pan*. Harper, 1986.

Goble, Paul. *Iktomi and the Buzzard*. Orchard, 1984.

Gorey, Edward. *The Doubtful Guest*. Harcourt, 1957.

Havill, Juanita. *The Magic Fort*. Houghton, 1991.

Heide, Florence Parry. *Sami and the Time of the Troubles*. Clarion, 1992.

Henwood, Simon. *The Troubled Village*. Farrar, 1991.

Joose, Barbara. *The Thinking Place*. Knopf, 1982.

Kurtz, Jane. *Trouble*. Gulliver, 1997.

Lee, Harper. *To Kill a Mockingbird*. Harper, 1960.

Lester, Julius. "What is Trouble?" In *The Knee-High Man and Other Tales*. Dial, 1972.

Noble, Trinka. *The Day Jimmy's Boa Ate the Wash*. Dial, 1980.

Prelutsky, Jack. *Rolling Harvey Down the Hill*. Greenwillow, 1980.

Rockwell, Thomas. *How to Eat Fried Worms*. Watts, 1973.

Root, Phyllis. *Aunt Nancy and Old Man Trouble*. Scholastic, 1989.

Sachar, Louis. *The Boy Who Lost His Face*. Knopf, 1989.

Seuss, Dr. *The Cat in the Hat*. (Houghton, 1957).

Spinelli, Jerry. *Maniac Magee*. Little, 2000.

Teague, Mark. *The Trouble with the Johnsons*. Scholasic, 1989.

Wahl, Jan. *Little Eight John*. Lodestar, 1992.

Films, Videos, and DVDs

Babe, directed by Chris Noonan. Universal, 1995. 91 minutes.

J.T. CBS, 1969. 51 minutes.

Leave It to Beaver: The Complete First Season, directed by Norman Abbot and Charles Barton. Univeral Home Entertainment, 2005. 25-minute episodes.

The Music Man, directed by Morton DaCosta. Warner, 1962. 151 minutes.

The Sandlot, directed by David Mickey Evans. Fox, 1993. 97 minutes.

Stand by Me, directed by Rob Reiner. Columbia, 1986. 87 minutes.

Sugar Cane Alley, directed by Euzhan Palcy. France, 1983. 103 minutes.

THEME 8:
Rain, River, and Sea··●

Water is such a natural theme to pursue with children because children are so drawn to it and so often engaged in water activities. At school young children will eagerly wait their turn at the water table where they can pour liquid from can to container and sneak in a few quiet splashes. At home they may delight in taking baths, and the tub can be a vessel for pretending and adventuring. This is why children identify with the book character *King Bidgood* (Wood), who refuses to get out of the tub and rule his kingdom. They, too, might prefer to escape from their realities or may just need some privacy and uninterrupted dreamtime.

As children grow older, water can become a source of both pleasure and mastery. A backyard creek or stream can stimulate children to construct dams and bridges or act out a hundred pirate dramas. All the while, they are learning to improvise, to problem solve, to be resourceful. They can become investigators on their excursions to the sea. Here there are clams to dig for, tides to watch, beach glass and shells to find and sort through. In learning to swim, they are challenged to develop specific skills and perhaps overcome certain fears. To swim successfully for the first time in deep water is to triumph and feel a leap in confidence. It is almost a sacred rite of passage—one that becomes a vivid, empowering memory.

Children's perceptions of water are ever changing. They may see it as joyful and energizing, or as scary and unsettling. Many times they will feel ambivalent. Whether skimming stones on the surface or wading in waist-high shallows, there is always the element of not knowing, of wonder and suspense. What might happen next? Will they find adventure, refreshment, or moments of genuine horror?

This exploration emphasizes the poetic and emotional dimensions of the theme and asks children to consider a number of questions. It sensitizes them to look carefully at their surroundings and to be more aware of visual details, movements, scents, and sounds. Through their writing, they might develop character sketches about beach people and how they are affected by the moods and rhythms of the sea. They may share original folktales that take place on or near the river. They may look at the impact of pollution and learn that even rivers and oceans can die. Hopefully, this journey will awaken and deepen their concerns about protecting the water, once they know that things must change.

Rain

What might be the texture of a summer's day when everyone is waiting for the rain? What causes the subtle changes in mood and tone? What heralds the rain's beginning? What are rain shadows, and how do rainbows form? Who invented the umbrella?

Children might want to discuss why stormy days have such an edge. Some children may want to find out about the rain cycle and how it is explained in science books as well as in folktales and myths.

From *Theme Play: Exciting Young Imaginations* by Gary Zingher. Wesport, CT: Libraries Unlimited. Copyright © 2006.

The first sparks of an electric sky can have a strong effect on children. For some, the rain brings pleasure and diversion. For others, wistfulness or even a feeling of deep despair may set in. Rain can be associated with mud hikes and splash fights or long gray days of feeling cut off and having to stay indoors.

A Rainy Day (Markle) offers a scientific look at the effects of rain. What are the reactions of various animals? Which animals stay outside? Which ones hide under the leaves? In *Rain Talk* (Serfozo), a young girl embraces the rain, delighting in its rhythms as it falls on various surfaces. Intently, she listens, wondering what each sound means.

Time of Wonder (McCloskey) shows two children's buoyant response to a cloudburst and their sweet surrendering. Set on an island as the sky begins to cloud, the book has a strong sense of immediacy. Through the illustrations, readers can see the changes in shadow and light and actually feel the buildup, the crescendo. "Now take a breath. It's raining on you!"

Who might be around to ease a child's fear of a rainstorm? Who could help a child remain calm when bolts of lightning become too vivid, and claps of thunder are loud and intense?

The grandparents described in *Stina* (Anderson), *Thunder Cake* (Polacco), and *Storm in the Night* (Stolz) all have a special touch—a natural ability to comfort a child during periods of stress. They know how to engage children, sometimes injecting a little humor and sometimes helping them confront their fears head-on. Whether taking a rain hike, finding ingredients for a cake, or swapping tales on a front porch swing, in each of these stories, a grandparent and grandchild are able to strengthen their bond and turn a scary episode into a heartfelt adventure.

What are some rain stories from different cultures? *Lazy Lion* (Hadithi) explains why the lion wanders the African plains unprotected when the big rains come. Lazy and arrogant, the lion orders smaller animals to build him a home, but, in the end, his bossy ways backfire. The lesson of this lion tale encourages children to be self-reliant and not just depend on others.

A second African tale, *Bringing the Rain to Kapiti Plain* (Aardema), introduces Ikpat, the hero, who pierces a cloud with a special arrow, stealing the rain and rescuing his people from drought. Without the rain, the grass would surely die, and so would the animals that need it for grazing.

The Andean myth *Llama and the Great Flood* (Alexander) illustrates the importance of dreams and in knowing the future. A llama dreams about a great flood and persists in warning his owner. Finally, the owner takes heed, leading his family to the highest mountain, where they can be safe and build a new world. This story makes clear why the mammal is so revered by the Quecha people of Peru.

Rain Player (Wisniewski) is an exciting Mayan tale about Pik, a daring and defiant boy, who challenges the Rain God to a game of pok-a-tok (a type of ball game) so he can end a terrible drought. In his quest to prepare for the game, he is aided by the Jaguar, the Quetzal, and Cenote, the sacred water. The heroic Pik is someone who is willing to take risks and pursue his own course of action.

In universal tales such as these, there are many common elements. The water and the sky are alive. Animals are highly valued, and often they can speak. There is a belief in dreams and prophecies. When people and animals have to deal with the extremes of a flood or a drought, sometimes heroes emerge to provide leadership and safety.

River

Where is the river the deepest, the widest? Where does the river bend? Where are the best river views? What animals depend on the river? What is the mood of the river at daybreak? Who takes care of the river? Who are the children who live nearby? What kinds of hideouts do they make? Do they have diving rocks or lookout points? Do they have secret ways of catching fish? What treasures might they find in or near the water?

The river is often a powerful force in books and films. Think of Huckleberry Finn (Twain) escaping on his raft with Jim or the surprised young hero in the film *Hope and Glory* marveling at a large number of leaping fish. Both of these scenes are exhilarating. Read once again Rat's ode to the river in *The Wind in the Willows* (Grahame). One can feel his enthusiasm, passion, and fine appreciation for his riverside way of life. "It's my world and I don't want any other. It's always got its fun and its excitement." But the river can turn from playful to menacing. It can offer freedom or obstruct someone's journey. It can soothe and heal or harm with its rough currents and white water.

How does the river challenge those who love to fish and canoe? *A River Dream* (Say) lyrically fuses dream and reality. A boy asleep in his bed imagines a river outside his house where he and his uncle are fishing. At the peak of his dream, he must decide whether or not to return a glimmering trout to the water. The book is flavored with the language of fishing. It is clear from the text that the uncle has a deep respect for both the fish and the river, and this he passes on to his nephew.

Three Days in a River in a Red Canoe (Williams) is an illustrated log of one girl's boating adventures with her mother, aunt, and brother. It describes how they work cooperatively and share the labor and the joy. As they travel down the Delaware River, they find crayfish, spot a great blue heron, encounter a waterfall, and camp out on an island. All this time, the river keeps winding and changing. The book is enhanced by maps, drawings, and instructions on tying knots and putting up a tent. It even includes recipes for making fruit stew and dumplings.

What are the river stories that are told in various cultures? "The Serpent's Bride" (Berger) is a Shangani tale from Africa. In this tale, the princess Timba marries a giant serpent for her own mysterious reasons. The story shows how the river is the vital center of tribal life, the source of all things important. What happens when the water becomes bewitched? Why does it dry up and disappear even when there are clouds and storms? This is a haunting tale with beautiful descriptive passages, especially of the river at night. It is about courage and love, about having faith and transcending one's fears. It has a strong heroine in Timba—one who is patient, intuitive, and risk taking.

Three Hispanic-themed books published by the Children's Book Press emphasize the power and character of the river. In the Mexican tale *The Woman Who Outshone the Sun* (Cruz), Lucia, a beautiful woman with the gift of magic, is exiled from a mountain village. Many distrust her because she is strange and different and feel compelled to drive her away. But the river has fallen in love with her, and when Lucia leaves, the river leaves too, flowing into her long, black hair along with the fishes and otters. Now the riverbed is dry and barren, and the people are devastated, regretting their ways. The story has a strong message about compassion and tolerance and a beautiful rejoicing scene when Lucia and the river return.

Atariba and Niguayona (Rohmer) is a legend from the Taino people of Puerto Rico. It tells about a young boy's quest to find the special fruit of a healing tree, so that he can save his best friend from dying. A problem arises when he must cross a "wide, deep river." Again in this story, the river is alive, responsive, and helpful.

In *Friends from the Other Side* (Anzoldua), the river serves as a vehicle for escaping poverty and as a barrier for separating two worlds. Crossing the Rio Grande promises a better life for Mexican families, but the conditions they find on the other side of the river are not so satisfactory. There are limited, low-paying jobs to compete for and border guards who must be avoided. This story involves a brave Mexican American girl who reaches out to and protects a Mexican immigrant boy. Their friendship helps to cushion the prejudice and name-calling that he experiences. The core of the book is about living with hardships and tensions and still maintaining one's dignity.

The title character in *Iktomi and the Ducks* (Goble), a Plains Indian story, is a trickster whose big plans always backfire. When he spies red berries in the river, he feels inspired to make berry soup, but a series of mishaps block him from his goal. Eventually, he realizes that the berries in the water are only a reflection.

Two picture books look at particular rivers from a historical point of view. *A River Ran Wild* (Cherry) tells about the Nashua River, beginning with its discovery by Native Americans. It documents the old story of progress and invention and how the river becomes poisoned when chemicals and wastes are dumped into the water. The book powerfully shows the rebirth of a dying river. It describes the efforts of environmentalists to revitalize it and offers a vision, a sense of hope, and a model for change.

Jane Yolen's *Letting Swift River Go* describes a transformation in which a river town is evacuated and drowned to prepare for a new reservoir. In this situation, how does one make peace with one's roots and memories? This is a personal account of a farewell boat ride—a lovely, lingering book about holding on and letting go.

Sea

What are the mysteries of the tides? What are the treasures of the shore? What do beachcombers prize the most? Who is Neptune? Who are the sirens, and how do they lure sailors to their death? What are ghost ships? Are there really sea serpents and sea monsters? How big are tidal waves? When might the sea be embracing and tranquil, and when might it be overwhelming and terrifying? When is the best time to dig for clams? How close do sharks come to shore?

The pull of the sea is powerful and magnetic. Images of boats at sea can sustain would-be sailors and occupy their dreams and fantasies. The pretend navigator in *And I Must Hurry for the Sea Is Coming In* (Mendoza) imagines sailing his own sailboat into the "spray singing sea." For him the sea represents vast open space, freedom, and high adventure. In reality, he is playing with his toy boat by an open hydrant on a city street.

The dream of the sea inspires the Native American boy in *Paddle-to-the-Sea* (Holling) to carve a model canoe that he hopes will journey to the ocean. It is his way of nourishing his dream and transporting himself, even if only vicariously.

What discoveries might one make on a hike along the shore? One might observe the odyssey of a hermit crab searching for a new home in which to hide in *Is This a House for a Hermit Crab?* (McDonald). The crab in question seeks refuge in a variety of places, but they always prove inadequate. The driftwood is too dark; the plastic pail is too deep. This slow, awkward borrower must find protection, or he is apt be eaten by the prickle pinefish, his natural enemy. Judith Rinard's *Along a Rocky Shore* is an information book that describes the members of the shoreline community—the sea slug, the rockfish, the kittiwake.

In *Where Does the Trail Lead?* (Albert), an African American boy follows the trail on Summertime Island. One can sense his liveliness and spirit in this animated and poetic book. He is often in motion—running, leaping, spreading his arms to imitate the geese. From time to time, he stops to inspect a tide pool or to spy on a family of rabbits. He ponders about what used to be as he glimpses a broken boat, old tires and tracks, and a ghost town of shanties. Wherever he wanders, he can feel the power of the sea.

What are the experiences of those who go fishing or searching for seafood? The Inuit girl in *The Very Last First Time* (Andrews) goes below the sea ice, for the first time without her mother, to search for mussels. This is an eerie, cavernous setting. What happens when her candle flame goes out? Will she be able to find the ice hole before the tide roars back? The elements of light and sound are critical in this story, and the author effectively captures Eva's moments of panic and desperation.

In a humorous vein, *The Eye of the Needle* (Sloat) has fun with the greedy character Amik, an Inuit boy with an endless appetite. He goes on a hunt to find food for himself and his grandmother and ends up devouring a needlefish, a hooligan fish, a salmon, a seal, a walrus, and a whale. Of course, he comes home bloated, tired, and empty-handed. He has a lot of explaining to do and must rely on the patience and wisdom of his grandmother.

What are the delights and concerns of children of island cultures? Lynn Joseph depicts the bright-colored world of Trinidad through poetry in *Coconut Kind of Day* and through short stories in *A Wave in Her Pocket.* Enjoy a snail race or a trip to the market, listen to the pulsating steel drums, meet the Coconut Man and the Palet Man and see their delicious display of treats, but beware of the Jumbi Man, who will scare you if you stay out in the dark. Both works reveal how the sea affects all aspects of island life, offering sea baths, tasty fish, and intense red sunsets. *Sugar Cane Alley*, a film set in Martinique in the 1930s, can further enrich an exploration of island cultures. The film has an extraordinary young hero, Jose, whose integrity and piercing intelligence sometimes shake up the adults in his world.

What are the hardships that one might endure at sea? Two historical novels document the horrors that can happen on sea journeys. In Paula Fox's *The Slave Dancer*, misery is reflected in the bleeding ankles of slaves and unhealthy, wretched latrines. How sad that a kidnapped boy named Jessie must use his gift for playing the fife in such a destructive way. He is the one who creates the music that slaves in chains must dance to, and he is disgusted by his role and abhors everything he sees.

In *A Boat to Nowhere* (Wartski) a Vietnamese grandfather and three children flee the new tyrannical regime in a small fishing vessel. Theirs is a turbulent journey of a small boat surviving the odds. Often they feel vulnerable and out of control as though "riding a horse gone mad." In both accounts, the fears of being punished or drowning always pervade.

Who are some of the mythical beings of the sea? In *The Seal Mother* (Gerstein), the title character can "shed her skin and become a woman." A fisherman witnesses her transformation, then steals her magic skin, promising to give it back in seven years if she will agree to marry him. This Scottish tale is about promises not kept. At the heart of the story is one boy's dilemma. Should he hold back, or should he help free his mother and risk losing her forever? The story is tinged with melancholy, for the good seal mother is so haunted by the music of the sea.

In *The Seashore Story* (Yashima), a Japanese fisherman saves a wounded turtle and is rewarded with a trip to a beautiful palace under the sea. But after days and then years of happy feasting, he starts to yearn for sunlight, for being in his own land among his own people. He craves to return to the shore, just as the seal mother craved to return to the sea.

What are the poisons that threaten the life of sea creatures? *Oceans in Peril* (Fine) examines toxic wastes and how plant and animal resources are being affected by them. It is a book that can provoke discussion and debate and stimulate children to think about what actions even they could take to educate others and protect the sea environment.

Creative Excursions

The River Rock School. With a simple fluid text and handsome, blue-toned woodcuts, *The Bear's Autumn* (Tejima) peeks in on a mother bear giving a fishing lesson to her eager cub. This book can be used as a springboard for dramatic play. Younger children, working in pairs or small groups, can create improvisations that take place at the River Rock School. In this imaginary setting, animals conduct a variety of classes. An otter teaches how to slide down a muddy bank. A beaver demonstrates the principles of dam building. A crow explains the art of scavenging.

Tall-Tale Writing. The Rag-and-Bone man, vividly etched in *The Rain Door* (Hoban), is a full-time rainmaker. This book could inspire younger and middle-grade children to concoct original stories about other rainmakers and cloud catchers in a whimsical, tall-tale style. They might want to create a procession of rainmakers who, with costumes and props, take turns revealing their secrets and methods.

A Rain Festival. Younger or middle-grade children could break into pairs or small groups to develop a special program. They would need several sessions to put this together. During the program, they could read aloud the beginning of *The Rain Babies* (Melmed), tell a version of "Stormalong," and share the two Native American rain poems from *The Trees Stand Shining*. One group could perform and then teach the "Mayim," an Israeli rain dance. Another group could present a fashion show of unusual umbrellas and rainwear. The Rag-and-Bone man could then appear with his cart and pretend-horse, serving small pieces of "thunder cake." The festival might begin with rain songs and close with everyone singing "Here Comes the Sun."

The Seashell People. Younger or middle-grade children can imagine themselves as tiny seashell people living safely in conch houses somewhere near the sea. They are good at fishing, use pieces of driftwood for making boats, and are always looking for pearls and beach glass. How do they deal with the problems of lobsters and high waves? What kinds of adventures and celebrations do they have? Children can develop their ideas into small-sized books with maps and illustrations.

....

Once a year the seashell people have a rodeo. They ride seahorses and catch cattlefish. They eat sea burgers and fish fries. They make music by hitting shell drums with crab legs, and use seaweed string for guitars.

Kenien L. Spann, age 9

It was noisy. Coming from a public beach ten feet away, there were shouts, screams, yells, and the usual noise of waves crashing on the rocks. In their seashell house, it was completely chaotic. Baby was crying. The twins were fighting. Father was pounding on a driftwood chair, and mother was eating a seaweed casserole. She grabbed it hungrily, not noticing the dark shadow that passed over her.

Chloe Kitzinger, age 8

....

A Riverside Choir. Middle-grade children with strong musical interests may wish to form a choir. They could learn and perform a medley of river songs. These might include spirituals, work songs, and the rousing folksongs of Pete Seeger. Some children may want to create their own songs, perhaps about Huck Finn's raft or Mike Fink's keelboat.

Creating Original River Tales. Middle-grade or older children could develop original tales that take place on or near the river. They would first need to think about the particular river in their story and be able to describe its images, smells, and sounds. What is the character of that river? What makes it unique? What is it like at different times of the day? They would then need to think about different scenarios and conflicts. What might happen when the river gets too high or too dry? What might happen when something scary emerges from the water?

Why might a river elf be gathering feathers and reeds? In other story lines, someone might be on a journey or quest, someone might be lost or hurt, someone might be trying to get across the river, or someone might be making a giant sculpture out of clay.

....

My river is very mysterious. It has no source. It dries out and then it fills up again. When you cup the water in your hands, it does not leak out, and won't even evaporate from the sun's heat. Not even I, the teller of this story, can tell you why this happens.

Mark Emmerich, age 10

....

Creating a Sea Environment. To celebrate the ocean, its beauty and resources, middle-grade or older children could transform a space into a giant sea environment. Murals of undersea life, pirate maps, and hanging stuffed paper fish can visually enhance this world. Divided into small groups, each group would develop a special exhibit or learning center. One group can create Little Atlantis, a model of the mythical city. Another group might create a puppet show in which sea

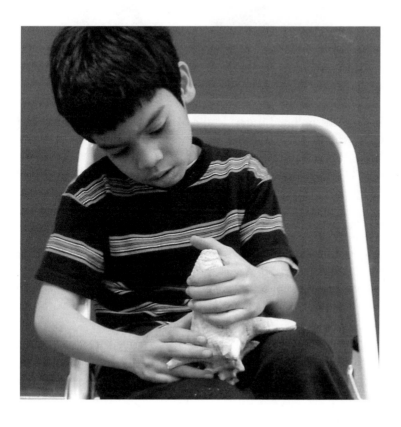

9-year-old David Valentin of Corlears School, telling the sea story *Bimwili and the Zimwi* (Aardema). Photographed by Bonnie Levine.

animals protest the polluted water. In the Moby Dick area, a costumed Captain Ahab could read from his journal and demonstrate how to use a harpoon. Biographies of Rachel Carson (Reef) and Jacques Cousteau (Reef) can be on display in a "heroes and heroines" corner. At the listening galley, visitors can enjoy sea chants, the songs of whales and dolphins, or an original island ghost story.

Beach People.   Middle-grade or older children could create beach characters through creative writing. Who are the beach people? Why do they come to the shore? What are their pleasures, frustrations, secrets, and dreams? What is the strange or powerful thing they discover or witness? These characters might include a poet, a sound collector, a sandcastle builder, a lighthouse keeper, or a crusty old pirate going to a reunion.

....

I am an artist. I go to the beach every evening at the twilight hour to watch the purple waves, to listen to the swish of the tides, and to get inspiration. I think the beach is the most beautiful place. Everything on it and all the sounds and smells are like a poem. When I paint the beach, I feel like my brush is writing down that poem with everything it creates on that canvas.

Eva Navon, age 10

....

In Years to Come. Older children could read and then dramatize Ray Bradbury's "All Summer in a Day." This futuristic short story describes a perpetually gray world, where it rains in seven-year cycles without the presence of any sunlight. It involves a group of children and a cruel, unforgivable act that occurs when the light finally shines through.

Resources

Books

Aardema, Verna. *Bimwili and the Zimwi*. Dutton, 1985.
Aardema, Verna. *Bringing the Rain to Kapiti Plain*. Dial, 1981.
Albert, Burton. *Where Does the Trail Lead?* Simon, 1991.
Alexander, Ellen. *Llama and the Great Flood: A Folktale from Peru*. Crowell, 1989.
Ancona, George. *Riverkeeper*. Macmillan, 1986.
Anderson, Lena. *Stina*. Morrow, 1989.
Andrews, Jan. *The Very Last First Time*. Atheneum, 1986.
Anzoldua, Gloria. *Friends from the Other Side*. Children's Book Press, 1993.
Baker, Jeannie. *When the River Meets the Sea*. Greenwillow, 1987.
Berger, Terry. "The Serpent's Bride," in *Black Fairy Tales*. Atheneum, 1969.
Carr, Terry. *Spill! The Story of Exxon Valdez*. Watts, 1991.
Cherry, Lynne. *A River Ran Wild*. Harcourt, 1992.
Conrad, Pam. *The Tub People*. Harper, 1989.
Cooper, Susan. *The Selkie Girl*. Macmillan, 1986.
Cruz, Alejandro. *The Woman Who Outshone the Sun*. Children's Book Press, 1991.
Fine, John. *Oceans in Peril*. Atheneum, 1987.
Fox, Paula. *The Slave Dancer*. Bradbury, 1973.
George, Jean. *Who Really Killed Cock Robin?* Harper, 1971.
Gerstein, Mordicai. *The Seal Mother*. Dial, 1986.
Goble, Paul. *Iktomi and the Ducks*. Orchard, 1989.
Grahame, Kenneth. *The Wind in the Willows*. Aladdin, 1989.
Hadithi, Mwenye. *Lazy Lion*. Little, Brown, 1990.
Hoban, Russell. *The Rain Door*. Crowell, 1986.
Holling, Holling. *Paddle-to-the-Sea*. Houghton, 1969.
Humphrey, Margo. *The River That Gave Gifts*. Children's Book Press, 1987.
Johnston, Tony. *Whale Song*. Putnam, 1987.
Jones, Hettie. *The Trees Stand Shining*. Dial, 1971.
Joseph, Lynn. *Coconut Kind of Day*. Lothrop, 1990.
Joseph, Lynn. *A Wave in Her Pocket*. Clarion, 1991.
Locker, Thomas. *Where the River Begins*. Dial, 1984.
Markle, Sandra. *A Rainy Day*. Orchard, 1993.

McCloskey, Robert. *Time of Wonder.* Viking, 1957.

McDonald, Megan. *Is This a House for a Hermit Crab?* Orchard, 1990.

Melmed, Laura. *The Rain Babies.* Lothrop, 1992.

Mendoza, George. *And I Must Hurry for the Sea Is Coming In.* Prentice-Hall, 1969.

Noble, Trinka. *Hansy's Mermaid.* Dial, 1983.

O'Dell, Scott. *Island of the Blue Dolphins.* Houghton, 1960.

Polacco, Patricia. *Thunder Cake.* Philomel, 1990.

Reef, Catherine. *Jacques Cousteau: Champion of the Sea.* Twenty-first Century, 1992.

Reef, Catherine. *Rachel Carson: The Wonder of Nature.* Twenty-first Century, 1992.

Rinard, Judith. *Along a Rocky Shore.* National Geographic, 1990.

San Souci, Robert. *Sukey and the Mermaid.* Macmillan, 1992.

Say, Allen. *A River Dream.* Houghton, 1988.

Scheer, Julian. *Rain Makes Applesauce.* Holiday, 1964.

Serfozo, Mary. *Rain Talk.* McElderry, 1990.

Shulevitz, Uri. *Rain Rain Rivers.* Farrar, 1969.

Sloat, Teri. *The Eye of the Needle.* Dutton, 1990.

Stock, Catherine. *Armien's Fishing Trip.* Morrow, 1990.

Stolz, Mary. *Storm in the Night.* Harper, 1988.

Tejima, Kelzaburo. *The Bear's Autumn.* Green Tiger, 1986.

Twain, Mark. *Huckleberry Finn.* Grosset, 1948.

Wartski, Maureen. *A Boat to Nowhere.* Westminster, 1980.

Waterton, Betty. *A Salmon for Simon.* Atheneum, 1980.

Williams, Vera. *Three Days in a River in a Red Canoe.* Greenwillow, 1981.

Wisniewski, David. *Rain Player.* Clarion, 1991.

Wood, Audrey. *King Bidgood's in the Bathtub.* Harcourt, 1985.

Yashima, Taro. *Seashore Story.* Viking, 1967.

Yashima, Taro. *Umbrella.* Viking, 1958.

Yolen, Jane. *Letting Swift River Go.* Little, 1992.

Films, Videos, and DVDs

Hope and Glory, directed by John Boorman. Columbia, 1987. 112 minutes.

The Night of the Hunter, directed by Charles Laughton. United Artists, 1955. 93 minutes.

Santiago's Ark. ABC, 1973. 47 minutes.

Sugar Cane Alley, directed by Euzhan Palcy. France, 1984. 103 minutes.

THEME 9:
Oddballs ....●

Two picture-book protagonists, Velvet from *Odd Velvet* (Whitcomb) and Wesley from *Weslandia* (Fleischman), are kindred spirits in the deepest sense. Both are attuned to nature and all its splendid offerings. Both see the world with a magical eye and approach each day with a sense of adventure. Inventive and resourceful, they are improvisers and transformers. Velvet involves others in creating a bedroom castle, and Wesley develops his own backyard civilization.

Because Velvet and Wesley are so inner-directed, they are oblivious to mainstream fads and styles and out of step with their peer groups. In being their true selves, they dare to be different, and this rubs others the wrong way. Velvet is ignored and isolated at school. Wesley is teased and tormented.

Velvet's classmates find her to be very peculiar. It bothers them that she would choose an old, ordinary dress to wear on the first day of school. It baffles them that she would bring her lunch in a paper bag rather than a shiny, colorful lunchbox. (She even eats plain, butter sandwiches.) And it confounds them that she would bring in a milkweed pod for Show-and-Tell, thinking it to be a special and wondrous thing.

But when Velvet, on a school bus outing, describes the morning that she was born and named, the richness and poetry of her words help create an extraordinary calm as others imagine a "world covered with a blanket of smooth, soft, lavender velvet."

A week later she moves her fellow students again, this time with her drawing of an apple that is so real and vivid–the kind of apple for both admiring and tasting. It is through her fresh and startling images that she begins to connect with her classmates, exciting their imaginations.

The clincher, though, is Velvet's birthday party. This is what really wins them over. At first they are surprised and disappointed when there are no clowns or magicians to entertain them. Instead, they learn to entertain themselves, as they become creators and castle makers. Working with face paint and glitter and wearing crowns, they achieve the royal look and speak the royal language while "jumping high off the bed into a blue blanket moat." At last Odd Velvet is valued and no longer maligned or misunderstood.

Wesley, too, knows quite a lot about being ostracized and not fitting in. His main contact with his peers is adversarial and involves them pursuing him with a vengeance, chasing him home each day after school. They hate the fact that he does not conform, that he refuses to wear their half-scalped hair style, and that he thumbs his nose at football, pizza, and soda.

When Wesley, as a summer project, decides to create his own staple food crop and his own civilization, his tormenters and neighbors are naturally curious. What is this weird guy up to now?

On day one of his ambitious venture, Wesley turns over the soil of his backyard plot and then, at night, waits for the winds, the seed bringers, to do their job. "Wesley found it thrilling to open his land to chance, to invite the new and unknown."

After a period of five days, a mysterious plant appears, and it grows unusually tall. Its magenta-colored fruit tastes like an "enticing blend of peach, strawberry, pumpkin pie, and flavors he had no name for." The root, rind, bark, fibers, and seeds provide him with all the materials he needs for making clothing and shelter and for fashioning a cup, a squeezing device, a flute, and a loom.

As the summer progresses, Wesley creates his own alphabet, number system, and sundial, while others become more and more intrigued. In the spirit of Tom Sawyer, Wesley cons his schoolmates into crushing the plant's seeds into oil and then charges them ten dollars a bottle for this combination of "insect repellent and suntan lotion." He then teaches them some rollicking games that require expert agility and balance—games where he is the one that excels. At summer's end, Wesley devises a scroll and makes his own ink so he can record the history of his civilization.

That fall, the newly empowered Wesley returns to school, not as a loner or loser, but as the inspirational leader of his schoolmates. Eagerly, they follow him in Wesley-style robes and hats, listen to his ideas, and emulate his ways.

Here is to the Velvets and the Wesleys of the world! Here is to the oddballs, the outcasts, the misfits, and the underdogs! Here is to those offbeat children who may be perceived as undesirable, the ones with "cooties," the ones who are singled out for being too dreamy, too goofy, too nerdy.

Sadly, others may dismiss these children without anyone really knowing them. They may be teased or simply tolerated. They may become the fodder for lunchtime gossip and may be exiled from informal playground games. Often they are labeled as "weird" or "uncool," and their reputation not only precedes them but also locks them in, limiting their possibilities for friendships.

This is why stories in which the oddball child ultimately triumphs are so sweet and compelling. How touching it is to hear Chibi, the shy and picked-on Crow Boy (Yashima), summon from his soul the haunting voices of crows, changing forever how he will be seen and regarded by those at his school. How moving it is to see Billy Elliot express his strongest feelings through his spirited dance steps, arousing something in his father, and forcing him to acknowledge Billy's potential.

Older children will feel empathy for such odd and unique characters as The Rough-Face Girl (Martin), The Flip-Flop Girl (Paterson), and Freak the Mighty (Philbrick). What sets them apart from others? Why do their siblings or peers react to them in such a negative manner? Are they off-putting or annoying? Are they, in some ways, threatening? Do these offbeat heroes and heroines see themselves as strange, or are they comfortable with who they are? Is being different a choice they have consciously made?

It is likely that all children, at particular times, think of themselves as odd or different, even the ones who are viewed as popular. All children have vulnerabilities, and all children have their shaky, awkward, agonizing moments. In childhood, it seems that one's self-esteem is always on the line.

But there are also children who choose to rebel, who refuse to adhere to any rigid code. They value the right to be different and may possess a certain strength and resolve. They may prefer reading Greek mythology or poetry rather than the latest popular chapter book. They may wear old-fashioned clothes. Some may come from families with alternative lifestyles.

Hopefully, these offbeat children will find family members, friends, teachers, and mentors who will encourage and support them, treat them generously and fairly, allow for their quirks and eccentricities, and recognize their special qualities and talents.

Eccentric Grown-ups

> I guess she does sound a little loony, but it's just because she does things her own way, and she doesn't give a hoot what people think. (*It's Like This Cat*, Neville)

Dave Mitchell, the compassionate hero of *It's Like This Cat* (Neville), has a tender spot for off-kilter characters like the woman he calls Aunt Kate. Other young people react to her bizarre fashion style, collection of orphan cats, and often-heard street soliloquies. They call her Crazy Kate the Cat Woman and take great pleasure in taunting her. Dave, on the other hand, finds her intriguing. Anyone like Aunt Kate, who thinks that green beans are unhealthy for you, has to be somewhat intact.

In fact, he is amused by her obsessions with tea and cottage cheese and is not put off by her little outbursts and tirades like when she hollers in the supermarket because the fruit is not ripe enough. Aunt Kate may have some weird notions and may be unusually vocal and opinionated, but Dave admires her tenacity and her courage to speak her mind.

He also knows that she has a special rapport with cats—that even the most timid and mangy cat will saunter over to her to receive a little affection. It is at Aunt Kate's where Dave first encounters Cat, the tomcat that will become his pet, soul mate, and prime listener.

When Aunt Kate learns through a telegram that her estranged brother, her only living relative, has died, Dave sees that she is unmoved by her loss. This eats at him as he realizes that she has "grown up loving only cats" but is almost indifferent toward other people. For the first time, he sees a lonely, fragile, and uncompromising woman who has retreated from the mainstream world.

Dave himself cherishes his adventures with his furry pal, but trusting and loving only Cat would never be enough. He knows he needs all kinds of friends in order to feel centered and complete. He needs their warmth and support and their diverse points of view.

Some of the most vivid and endearing characters in books and films are those eccentric types of grown-ups who stand out in a crowd because of their strange demeanor, quirky habits, or offbeat pursuits. Often they may appear a little disconnected and out of place. Yet many have remarkable gifts and insights and may offer sweet melodies, stimulating riddles, and enticing stories.

Think of Old Joseph in *All the Magic in the World* (Hartmann), a connoisseur of junk, who creates wonderful things out of string and soda can rings that he keeps in his tin. Children are enthralled when he makes string art pictures of a cup and saucer and a horse and transforms ordinary soda can tops into bracelets and chains.

Think of Aunt Ippy, the title character in *Aunt Ippy's Museum of Junk* (Greenblatt), who also sees junk as "treasure for the imagination." This woman is a force of nature, an unconventional dynamo, ecologically minded and wildly dressed. She celebrates her love for junk through her overflowing museum where a visiting child can touch everything, try out the new Roto Spinner, or rummage through the Chamber of Odds and Ends or the Grand Parlor of Scraps.

Think of The Dunkard (Selden), who is totally committed to the art of dunking and likes to dunk spaghetti strands into sauce and bread into pea soup. For him, dunking is not a hobby. It is his passion, and purpose, and reason for being, and he always dunks with style and panache.

Think of Willie Wonka (Dahl), a first-class oddball, who stays close to the heart of childhood and speaks the language of chocolate. Think of Alice Rumphius (Cooney), who makes it her mission to plant lupine seeds near hollows and highways everywhere to make the world a brighter, lovelier place. Think of the Chicken Man (Pinkwater) and his puffed-up white hen, entertaining passengers on the city bus with their medley of vaudeville tricks. Think of a wanderer named Ty (Walters), a man with few coins and possessions, yet a man with magical rhythms. When he puts on his impromptu concerts, playing all the instruments himself, he brings joy wherever he travels.

On the other hand, having an oddball parent or caretaker can, at times, make a child feel utterly embarrassed. How does a child explain their behavior when friends come over to visit?

In *Weird Parents* (Wood), the main character has to deal with a mother who loves to tell others about his stick-out bellybutton and a father who likes to perform the "chicken dance" while they are waiting in line at the movies. And even worse, as audience members, these two parents laugh at all the wrong moments, and they laugh with big, boisterous laughs, annoying and offending everyone around them.

Amy, the uprooted heroine in the film *Fly Away Home*, must learn to live with her inventor father in Canada after her mother is killed in a car accident. She feels awkward around him and is not sure what to make of his "harebrain schemes" and scattered, unconventional lifestyle. Only when she tries to raise a flock of orphaned geese does she begin to see and value his kindness and resourcefulness.

A dilemma for Nick, the precocious young adult in the film *A Thousand Clowns*, is that he genuinely enjoys the antics of the nonconformist Murray, his uncle and caretaker. Nick does not mind that Murray clutters their apartment with junkyard eagles or likes to holler out the window at the neighbors or carry on about the joys of being unemployed. And Nick especially loves it when they play their ukuleles and try out new impersonations. (Nick can do a terrific Peter Lorre.) The problem is that Murray never takes anything seriously. He is committed to the carefree, spontaneous life, and Nick worries that he will never find another job.

Curious Places

In visiting worlds depicted in books and films, children may be struck by the number of strange and nonsensical places. In these unusual settings, the rules of logic and common sense may not apply. Oddities become the norm, and eccentric behaviors are commonplace. Those who live in these places may seem silly or foolish, and their approach to life a little baffling, but there may be something familiar and endearing about the ways they carry on, struggle, and try to make sense of things.

Children might enjoy examining some of these neighborhoods, lands, and villages. What makes them unusual? How do the people in these places interact with each other? What are the conflicts that occur, and how are they resolved?

What follows are short descriptions of five curious places. To enter these worlds as travelers and observers, children will need to bring their sense of humor and imagination with them.

The Land of Point.   In the Land of Point, described in the movie *The Point,* every person has a pointed head, and all the buildings have pointed entrances. The barbershop is pointed, and the baker makes pointed bread. There are points on the farmer's crops, and the artist paints only points on his canvas. The chief activity in this town, obviously, is point making, and "that's the way life was," and that is how the people liked it.

But when Oblio is born, a baby without a point—a "no point," a "roundhead"— this proves threatening to the others. Even his parents are quite concerned. As this unique boy, with the help of his dog Arrow, becomes the champion of triangle toss, his victory is double-edged because he alienates his rival, the son of the count. Soon after, he is exiled and banished to the Pointless Forest. Does Oblio really need a point on his head to have a point? What does he learn on his odyssey?

Itching Down.   In Itching Down, depicted in the book *The Giant Jam Sandwich* (Lord), four million wasps create a panic by disrupting farmers and picnickers alike with their irritating buzzes and infuriating dives. The villagers feel helpless, frazzled, vexed, and perplexed. When they meet with Mayor Muddlenut in the village hall, it is Bap the Baker who comes up with a wild solution. He suggests that they make a giant jam sandwich and trap the wasps inside. After all, wasps cannot resist the sweetness of strawberry jam.

But where will the villagers bake this huge, building-sized loaf of bread? How then will they move it, and how will they slice it? Well, it turns out that the people of Itching Down are first-rate problem solvers, clever and ingenious. By cooperating and laboring hard, they are able to triumph over adversity and create a new wasp-free society.

Liberty Street.   In the extremely clean and orderly place called Liberty Street, General Pinch and his wife monitor the neighborhood (with binoculars, no less) to make certain that things remain quiet and homogeneous. The Pinches are very vigilant and hate any kind of playfulness or spontaneity. If they see children engaged in pretend games or party activities, the general will seize his bullhorn and threaten to "call in the army." Conformity is his watchword. Music and laughter will not be tolerated.

When the Araboolies (Swope) move to Liberty Street, there goes the neighborhood. The general and his uptight wife are appalled and disgusted. They do not know what to make of the garish vehicle they see pulling in—a kind of chaos-mobile, a commotion-on-wheels.

The number of Araboolies and their menagerie of pets, including anteaters and sloths, truly repel them. Furthermore, the Araboolies are multicolored, speak a different language, glow in the dark, and even sleep out in the yard. Their manner is outrageous, and their spirit is contagious. At last, the children of Liberty Street, inspired by their new neighbors, are beginning to have a little fun.

Mortified, the general calls for the army on his walkie-talkie. "Attack Liberty Street at dawn!" How does a little girl named Joy organize the children of Liberty Street to overcome this intolerant bully? How is this story really a fable about prejudice and the right to be different?

The Land of Yooks and Zooks.   In another conflicted place, this one divided by a great stonewall, the always itchy-to-argue Yooks and Zooks go to battle over the proper way to eat their bread. The Zooks prefer to eat their bread "with the butter side down." The Yooks insist that one should eat bread "with the butter side up."

This difference of opinion leads to a great schism between them, a lack of trust, and the inevitable blaming, name-calling, and displays of bravado. Border patrols are set up; slingshots are fired.

Soon the weapons get bigger and more inventive. One is called the Kick-a-Poo Kid, and another is called the Eight-Nuzzled, Elephant-Toted Boom-Blitz. The drums of war begin to beat as the Patriotic Song Girls bellow out, "Oh, be faithful! Believe in the butter!"

This wonderfully satirical work entitled *The Butter Battle Book* (Seuss) pokes fun at the big war machine and how it escalates and blinds people from simply using their common sense to find reasonable, nonviolent solutions. It is a funny and provocative tale, both outrageous and insightful.

The Village of Chelm.   Stories about the village of Chelm are very popular in Jewish folklore. The people of Chelm have an odd way of reasoning, and that is part of their humor and charm. In fact, one could say The Children of Chelm (Adler) have very loving parents who try to provide them with the essentials of a good and simple life. But because they are fools, these grown-ups blunder a lot while trying hard to improve the quality of their lives.

For example, when the children complain about having to bathe each week in the raw and chilly river, the adults decide that they should take a year's worth of baths in just one day. Imagine fifty baths in one short period. This clever plan, they think, will surely curtail the children's whining and moaning.

Another time, after the men of Chelm carry large numbers of heavy stones down the hill to build a new school, a child explains that they could have simply rolled the stones down the hill and prevented all that stress, sweat, and unnecessary labor. These men are so impressed by the child's observation that they carry the stones back up the hill and this time release them from the top. They are feeling incredibly wise, for they have found a shortcut—a time-saving and modern method.

Creative Excursions

Imagine a Town. Middle-grade or older children, after viewing *The Point* or reading *The Araboolies of Liberty Street* (Swope), could, in the session that follows, imagine a strange and wacky town where people behave in an unusual manner. They could choose a name for the town, then a motto and symbol. Next, in small groups, they could draw a map of the area, develop its rules or laws, and design a banner or flag.

In later sessions, children, again in small groups, could create the town's charter and history. Some could dramatize a conflict in the town through a simulated town meeting. Others might want to construct, in miniature, the town hall and the town's main street.

The following are examples of eccentric towns and were developed with 10- and 11-year-olds in library sessions at a school in Manhattan.

- In *Egg Town*, the citizens are always trying to develop the perfect omelet. Lovely little gardens are developed in eggshell cartons, and the museum offers an exhibit of eggshell collages. The worst thing to be called in Egg Town is a "rotten egg" and the people like their weather sunny-side up. Both children and grown-ups drive around in fancy egg-mobiles, and when the traffic gets thick, they call it a "scramble."

- In *Harmony Heights*, the townspeople never quarrel or say mean things to each other, and no one ever spoils the peace. The biggest conflict that happened here involved the choirmaster forgetting to send the bandleader a "you're welcome" card after the bandleader had sent him a "thank you" note. In Harmony Heights, whenever people come together, they begin to jam. Everyone in the town is a member of the glee club, the barbershop quartet, the whistler's choir, or the big bassoon band. The mayor, herself, can play fourteen instruments.

- In *Duckburg*, the people do the "duck walk" each day on the way to school and work, and they use duck feathers as currency. The favorite game is "Duck, Duck, Goose," and the movie *Duck Soup* is shown every Friday night at the Daisy Duck Cinema. There are 200 copies of *Make Way for Ducklings* (McCloskey) in the town library. When things are going good in the town, the people like to say, "Everything is just ducky."

- In *Secretville*, everybody spends the day telling secrets, and if you wander into this town, they whisper things in your ear. Spies and secret agents are the town's heroes and heroines, especially Briar Cudgeon (Colfer) and Harriet the Spy (Fitzhugh). All the people, including the children, write only in invisible ink, and the waiters at the town restaurant will not tell you what is on the menu because that is a secret, too.

• In *Sonnetville*, a self-absorbed king begins each morning by announcing on his royal broadcast what colors people should wear and who can sleep late on that particular day. He makes all of his announcements in rhyme. He then spends the rest of the morning composing sonnets and verse. Each afternoon he recites these by the fountain in his garden. Each of his poems is frivolous and clichéd, but the people of Sonnetville love them, and find them to be moving and profound.

The King's Bee Poem

I see a bee,
A big buzzing bee.
The yellow part tells me one thing.
The black part tells me two things.
I am happy.
I am humble;
I am here.
That bee speaks to me.
And that is why I am the King.

Oliver Button Buttons. Younger children could listen to and dramatize *Oliver Button Is a Sissy* (DePaola). They could then discuss the reasons his peers teased him so relentlessly. Is there anything wrong with a boy like Oliver Button who enjoys picking flowers and playing dress-up or a girl who likes climbing rocks or woodworking? Are there still expectations about how boys and girls each should behave? Children could honor this young tap dancer, who is so open about his interests, by making paper buttons to wear on their shirts. These might say, "Here's to Oliver," "Be Yourself," or "Oliver Button is a hero!"

The Runaway Wasps. After listening to the story *The Giant Jam Sandwich* (Lord), younger children could create drawings, stories, or flipbooks about the three wasps that escaped from Itching Down. How far did they travel, and where did they go?

The Land of Opposites. After listening to the story *Through the Magic Mirror* (Browne), younger children could develop their own picture books in which they enter a topsy-turvy world—a place like the mirror world in the book where a dog is walking a man with a collar and a frightened cat is being chased by a gang of mice.

Dunking Day. To celebrate *The Dunkard* (Selden), younger or middle-grade children could develop their own styles of dunking—perhaps the rodeo dunk, the disco dunk, the dainty dunk, and the cheerleader dunk. They could design and hand out "Dunk with Dignity" buttons and write their own dunking poems. For refreshments, they could dunk apples into honey, mini-pancakes into maple syrup, and donuts into chocolate milk.

The Odd Duck Auxiliary.   Pairs of children could choose an eccentric grown-up from a book and decide who would be the character and who would be the presenter. In a special celebration, each presenter would share their character's story and then introduce their character, who would either perform or teach something to the others. Aunt Ippy (Greenblatt) might demonstrate a few of her inventions and instruct others on how to construct junk towers. The Song and Dance Man (Ackerman) might perform one of his vaudeville routines and talk about a few of the costumes or props in his trunk. The Lorax (Seuss) could lecture about ecology and help others design their own tree houses. Finally, in a quiet ceremony, each presenter would initiate his or her grown-up into the Odd Duck Auxiliary by having the grown-up sign the Odd Duck Membership Log.

Oddballs on Trial.   Middle-grade children, through roleplaying, could create mock trials to decide if punishment is warranted for either of these small-town culprits.

• The disagreeable and disgruntled Old Sneep in Alto, Ohio, who tried to disrupt the homecoming of Colonel Carter by deliberately slurping on his lemon and paralyzing the lips of the musicians in the Alto Brass Band.
• The mean-spirited Grinch in Who-ville who tried to sabotage Christmas by stealing stockings, presents, ribbons, and wrappings. This notorious act was actually witnessed by Cindy Lou Who, who is now willing to testify against Mr. Grinch.

Two Against the World.   What happens when two odd or alienated children find each other and develop a friendship? How does this ease their loneliness? Do these relationships always work out? Middle-grade children could dramatize scenes from chapter books that explore this theme. What happens to Jennifer and Elizabeth in *Jennifer, Hecate, Macbeth, William McKinley, and Me, Elizabeth* (Konigsburg), to Mongoose and Weasel in *The Library Card* (Spinelli), to Freak and Max in *Freak the Mighty* (Philbrick)? What are the tensions and turning points in these relationships? How do these individuals complement each other?

Introducing Little Man Tate.   Older children could view this film and discuss what it might be like to be a 7-year-old genius and to go to a special school far away from home. How is he perceived and treated by others? Is he able to fit in and develop friendships? What does he worry about? Why are young intellectuals often called nerds and geeks? What gender issues tie into this theme? In any school is a "brainy" girl more likely to feel out of place than a "brainy" boy? Why are there so many prejudices against the so-called smart kids? Has this changed now that Bill Gates and Steven Spielberg have emerged as "real life" heroes and so many children aspire to be computer experts and film directors? Have the Harry Potter books dispelled some of these prejudices?

Resources

Books

Ackerman, Karen. *The Song and Dance Man*. Knopf, 1988.
Adler, David A. *The Children of Chelm*. Bonin, 1979.
Barrett, Judi. *Cloudy with a Chance of Meatballs*. Scholastic, 1978.
Browne, Anthony. *Through the Magic Mirror*. Greenwillow, 1976.
Colfer, Eoin. *Artemis Fowl: The Arctic Incident*. Miramax, 2002.
Cooney, Barbara. *Miss Rumphius*. Viking, 1982.
Dahl, Roald. *Charlie and the Chocolate Factory*. Knopf, 1985.
DePaola, Tomie. *Oliver Button Is a Sissy*. Harcourt, 1979.
DePaola, Tomie. *Strega Nona*. Simon, 1975.
Estes, Eleanor. *The Hundred Dresses*. Harcourt, 1944.
Fitzhugh, Louise. *Harriet the Spy*. Harper, 1964.
Fleischman, Paul. *Weslandia*. Candlewick, 1999.
Greenblatt, Rodney. *Aunt Ippy's Museum of Junk*. Harper, 1991.
Hamilton, Virginia. *The Planet of Junior Brown*. Aladdin, 1971.
Hartmann, Wendy. *All the Magic in the World*. Dutton, 1993.
Konigsburg, E. L. *Jennifer, Hecate, Macbeth, William McKinley, and Me, Elizabeth*. Atheneum, 1967.
Lawson, Robert. *Ben and Me*. Little, 1939.
Lord, John Vernon. *The Giant Jam Sandwich*. Houghton, 1972.
MacDonald, Betty. *Mrs. Piggle-Wiggle*. Scholastic, 1997.
Martin, Rafe. *The Rough-Face Girl*. Putnam, 1992.
McCloskey, Robert. *Lentil*. Scholastic, 1968.
McCloskey, Robert. *Make Way for Ducklings*. Viking, 1941.
McLerran, Alice. *Roxaboxen*. Lothrop, 1991.
Neville, Emily. *It's Like This, Cat*. Harper, 1963.
Paterson, Katherine. *The Flip-Flop Girl*. Lodestar, 1994.
Philbrick, Rodman. *Freak the Mighty*. Blue Sky, 1993.
Pinkwater, Daniel. *Lizard Music*. Dodd, 1976.
Selden, George. *The Dunkard*. Harper, 1968.
Seuss, Dr. *The Butter Battle Book*. Random, 1984.
Seuss, Dr. *How the Grinch Stole Christmas*. Random, 1957.
Seuss, Dr. *The Lorax*. Random, 1971.
Spinelli, Jerry. *The Library Card*. Scholastic, 1997.
Swope, Sam. *The Araboolies of Liberty Street*. Potter, 1990.
Walters, Mildred. *Ty's One-Man Band*. Four Winds, 1980.
Whitcomb, Mary. *Odd Velvet*. Chronicle, 1998.
Wood, Audrey. *Weird Parents*. Dial, 1990.
Yashima, Taro. *Crow Boy*. Viking, 1955.
Yolen, Jane. *Tea with the Old Dragon*. Boyds, 1998.

Films, Videos, and DVDs

Alice in Wonderland. Disney, 1951. 75 minutes.
Billy Elliott, directed by Stephen Daltry. Universal, 2001. 111 minutes.

Cheaper by the Dozen, directed by Walter Lang. Fox, 1950. 85 minutes.
Duck Soup, directed by Leo McCarey. Universal, 1933. 72 minutes.
Fly Away Home, directed by William Wyler. Columbia, 1968. 155 minutes.
Hans Christian Andersen, directed by Charles Vidor. MGM, 1952. 116 minutes.
The Point, directed by Fred Wolfe. Vestron, 1971. 74 minutes.
A Thousand Clowns, directed by Fred Coe. United Artists, 1965. 118 minutes.
The Wizard of Oz, directed by Victor Fleming. MGM, 1939. 101 minutes.

THEME 10:
Bedtime Rituals and Nighttime Journeys·····················●

In the journeys of children, how a day ends is extremely important. If there is a feeling of closure and of tying loose ends, children will feel relaxed and satisfied. The rituals of bedtime can ease children into the night and prepare them for their sleep. In *No, David!* (Shannon), a fiendish little boy, now in bed, finally hears some kind words from his mother. This reassures him of her unconditional love, no matter how many things he broke, or how many times he disobeyed. Every night these two clean the slate, hoping to begin anew.

Bedtime Rituals

The lucky, contented girl in Jan Ormerod's textless *Moonlight* has two parents guiding her through the rituals of bedtime. Feeling unrushed and cared for, she can take time to launch her homemade boat in the bathtub and to later brush her doll's reddish yarn hair. When she has trouble falling asleep, she can ask for a drink of water or get some extra cuddling from her father. On some nights, she may bring a book with her to the corner of the couch in the living room and do a little pre-bedtime reading nestled close to her mom.

Through the structure her parents have established, this critical part of the day becomes a calming, pleasurable experience. Both parents are attuned to their daughter's needs, partly because they are dealing with only one child. They are able to give and take and invest equal care, if not always equal energy.

Sometimes children dread the night. They begin to feel isolated after the lights go out and others in the room have fallen to sleep. They feel a loss of control. They are less clothed, less protected, and there is no one with whom to chat. At this hour they may be forced to confront their fears about being separated from parents or encountering a stranger or a monster. Whatever they are storing inside may begin to surface, for there are no more distractions—just the stillness and the darkness.

The young boy in *There's a Nightmare in My Closet* (Mayer) struggles with going to sleep, for he worries about a monster creeping close to his bed. When he finally takes charge and confronts the beast, he sees that his nightmare is a big, gawky, timid thing with two ridiculous baby teeth and large floppy ears. Relieved, he then becomes his nightmare's protector, the one who soothes it and tucks it under the blanket.

Bedtime rituals have a cumulative power for they connect the nights together. They promise safety and security and provide a sense of continuity and order. In families, there is a rich variety of bedtime rituals: reading stories aloud, making up stories, singing lullabies, saying prayers, counting sheep, giving back rubs, looking for wishing stars and making wishes, listening to night sounds, releasing fireflies, playing word games, asking riddles, and telling jokes. There are also the simple, comforting routines of drinking milk, eating a snack, making a last trip to the bathroom, closing the closet door, pulling the curtain, turning on the nightlight, and tucking in the teddy bear.

From *Theme Play: Exciting Young Imaginations* by Gary Zingher. Wesport, CT: Libraries Unlimited. Copyright © 2006.

Children can be so comfortable with their particular routines that if roles are reversed and they become the caretakers, they know exactly what to do. In *Tucking Mommy In* (Loh), Sue and her sister Jenny help put their working mother to bed when they sense how tired she is. Adept at telling stories, Sue concocts a funny tale about the family cat. She, like her mother, has strong nurturing instincts and values this chance to lend her support.

The power of telling stories as an important bedtime ritual is illustrated in *Tell Me a Story, Mama* (Johnson). A young girl loves hearing her mother's vignettes about childhood—captivating tales about a bullfrog, a train ride, and a hollering lady. She sees in these tales a girl very much like herself, and she can identify with her, root for her, and join her in the telling. This sacred time each night has become a comforting, eagerly awaited activity. The stories not only give her a vivid sense of her mother as a child but also connect her to her family's history.

Similarly, in *Knots on a Counting Rope* (Martin, Jr.), a Native American grandfather and his blind grandson deepen their bond each night while sitting around a campfire. Together, they tell the epic story of the boy's name and identity and about his love for wild horses. In another ritual, after the story is completed, the grandfather ties a knot on a counting rope to prepare the boy for the grandfather's eventual death. The knots reinforce their love and values. They represent the grandfather's legacy and the boy's growing confidence as both a young man and a storyteller. "When the rope is filled with knots, you will know the story by heart and can tell it yourself."

The father in *The Baseball Star* (Arrigg, Jr.) loves the storytelling ritual as much as his son does. It enables him to sharpen his imagination. He likes to spin tall tales like the one about how the brightest star is really his homerun ball hit off the obnoxious Killer McGrew that is "still traveling in outer space." Through his storytelling, he can express his outrageous sense of humor and share his childhood passions and interests.

Many children are soothed to sleep by the rhythmic cadences of a poem or the hypnotic melodies of a song. The lullaby *Hush!* (Ho) has a quieting effect with its gently pleading tone. A mother in Thailand takes on all the animals nearby, from the mosquito to the water buffalo, as she tries to protect the silence so her baby will fall asleep. "Hush! Who's that weeping in the wind?" she demands to know. "Hush! Who's that leaping by the well?" Her voice is forceful and low as she begs and cries and scolds.

How do children adapt when they are spending the night at the home of a relative or friend? How might the routines be different?

For Jenny, in *I Dance in My Red Pajamas* (Hurd), sleeping over at her grandparents is a joyful, spirited occasion. She loves collecting logs for the fireplace and is enchanted by the embers and flames. When her Granny plays the piano, Jenny begins to dance in her red pajamas. Soon she is partnering with her grandpa, stepping high and do-si-doing. The night culminates with a piggyback ride upstairs.

Ira, the anxious hero in *Ira Sleeps Over* (Waber), obsesses about his first night away from home and whether he should bring his teddy bear. He wants to impress his friend, Reggie, and convey a cool image, but it is his bear that helps him to deal with the darkness. Sleeping away from home is kind of scary because he does not know what to expect. Will there be some kind of snack? Will there be a nightlight? Will the bathroom be close by or far away?

Although bedtimes can be mellow, they can also be rushed and chaotic. Children do not always go gently into the night. Sometimes they are resistant. When parents are tired and preoccupied, children may feel shortchanged. Friction develops, and the bedroom can become a battleground. Words turn sour, and tempers flare. The parent's level of patience and tolerance is tested by the child's feistiness and will.

Children can be ingenious in their stalling tactics. Their goal is to extend the bedtime, to stretch it out in whatever devious ways they can. The exasperated parent may have to contend with any number of those why-I-am-out-of-bed-again excuses from their charged-up youngster. "I'm thirsty!" "I hear a buzzing thing!" "Eddie's snoring." "I think there is a chicken under my mattress." Even worse, parents may have to deal with refrigerator raids and nonstop pillow fights.

One of Bill Cosby's hilarious, on-target routines about growing up in Philadelphia captures how bedtime took its toll on his disgruntled father. In the routine, two bickering brothers turn each bedtime into a whine fest and war zone, where teasing is rampant, and big, juicy, provocative lies are told with just the right scary spin. All kinds of loud and strange noises erupt, and they travel into their father's room, puncturing his peace. Undoubtedly, these episodes become ritualized, with the chagrined father never getting more than a few winks of sleep.

The six scouts at Camp Badger feed off each other's fears after their counselor abruptly announces "Lights Out!" (Himmelman). This bedtime is a fiasco, as anxieties escalate and flashlights beam. "Is there really an eyeball on the ceiling?" they wonder. "Will it hypnotize them?" "Will giant mosquitoes drink all their body fluids?" Wound-up and jittery, these campers have no intention of sleeping now. If only their counselor had tried first to settle them in with a camp song like "Kum Ba Ya" or a quiet, involving story.

Observing bedtime rituals can help children feel in control. It can relax and sustain them and ease their anxieties. Each bedtime, though, has a life of its own, with its particular set of variables. The child may have extra energy, while the parent may feel listless and exhausted. Outside elements may come into play—the wind and the cold, the lightning and thunder, or the excessive humidity. In these situations, bedtime can be tense and prolonged, even tortuous and wrenching.

When bedtime works, however, it can be the most extraordinary part of the day, a time for intimacy and reflection. It enables a parent and child to touch base, look back on the day that is ending, and anticipate the day that is coming. In this nightly forum a child is able to raise any hopes or concerns and share what he or she is excited or worried about. After a calamitous day, a parent and child can finally laugh and release their emotions, knowing that they have somehow survived it together. Now they can let it all go and not have to carry any feelings of anger or disappointment.

Nighttime Journeys

> The wind lashed out against his fire,
> Beating it,
> Killing it,
> So he had to start again.
>
> "Oh, light, please come," he begged.
> The sounds around him
> Grew fierce and shrill,
> And he smelled the breath of night creatures.

Children can identify with the idea of being lost in the night and having to somehow survive. What will they do for shelter? Are they able to build a fire? How will they deal with their fears and anxieties? What might help them feel safe and protected?

When children journey into the night, their vision is less clear so they must listen more carefully. Some sounds will be comforting to them; others will be mysterious, even disturbing. They may hear the wind at play, the hissing of a steam pipe, or the soulful cry of a saxophone.

Most young travelers will be drawn to any source of light: a lamppost, a lighthouse, a spotlight, the flickering lights of fireflies, or the dazzling lights of a harbor or bridge. Sometimes the moon and stars will illuminate their path and provide them with a feeling of calmness.

All these sounds and lights help create the moods of the night, and each night has its own unique character, its own combination of elements. Some nights are tranquil. Some are eerie and mystical. Others can be thunderous and raging.

Children who go hiking and traveling in the night may get to know its secrets and surprises. Over time, they will begin to feel at home in this world and move around with self-assurance and ease. They may become true discoverers, puzzling over unusual shadows and delighting in the morning mist. Some may find out if there really is a snipe or a moonbird. Others may encounter a bat hunting for food or a bright-eyed fox silently crossing a country road.

Night Ride (Karlin) and *The Moon Is Following Me* (Heckman) each capture the excitement of a child traveling at night by car. Billy, in the first book, is impressed with the lights of an amusement park and sports stadium. As he and his mother drive away from the city, the sky becomes brighter and clearer, and he is able to spot a deer and a wishing star. The little girl in the second book obsesses about the big-faced moon. She feels a playful and personal connection with it as it pops out, then disappears. Sometimes the moon is reflected in the waters of the night. Often it is elusive, but, to her relief, it always returns.

The bond between grandmother and granddaughter in *When I Go Camping with Grandma* (Bauer) is strengthened by their love and appreciation of the outdoors. They both respond to the poetry of the night world and its images of a fat marshmallow turning brown, "tree bones in the lake," and a heron in flight. As they set up their tent and go kayaking and fishing, the granddaughter is absorbing everything. She is eager to receive her grandmother's gifts—her skills and her knowledge.

The father and daughter in *Owl Moon* (Yolen) go on a quest at night to see the great horned owl. This is the daughter's first such journey, and it is not an easy one. She must be very quiet, and, like her dad, she is learning to be remarkably patient.

At times, though, she feels cold, and other times she feels tired. She worries about the enormous shadows around her, but her father's hand helps her to feel more relaxed. Suspense builds when they come to a clearing where her father calls out, mimicking the sound of the great horned owl. Will the owl call back? Will she actually get to see it lift off and "pump its great wings"? And will the owl understand that they have come to pay their respects, to witness its power and beauty?

Sometimes whole families journey into the night to celebrate a special holiday. The Mexican family in *Day of the Dead* (Johnston) brings with them foods like empanadas and mole along with candles and marigolds. Excitedly, they join with other families weaving through the village and up the hill to the graveyard to be reunited with loved ones. This is a night of rituals, festive and communal. And it is a night for singing and dancing, for offering gifts and sharing memories.

Extraordinary things often seem to happen in the night, perhaps because of the mood and atmosphere and unexpected sounds and lights. When children journey in the night, there is always the element of suspense, the possibility of a great surprise.

In *The First Starry Night* (Isom) Jacques, a young French boy, becomes quite attached to the artist Vincent van Gogh, who lives in his boarding house, and the two often take walks together. Vincent teaches Jacques to be a careful observer of the natural world, to pay close attention to its colors and shadows.

In one of their outings, they venture into the night so that Vincent can paint the stars. It is Jacques's job to hold the candles for him, but Jacques is feeling drowsy and falls asleep. When he wakes up, he is amused to see candles sticking out of Vincent's headband, "his hat glowing like a strange birthday cake." What a magical and historical night it is—a night of creation, a night when Vincent van Gogh captures the stars on his canvas.

When Lilly, the heroine in *The Whale's Song* (Sheldon), leaves her bedroom at night, she runs all the way to the shore, where she is serenaded by five or six magnificent whales. In her nightgown, high up on the bank, she hears the whales calling her name.

Well, this is real, and her grandmother was right. These whales are "wondrous creatures," "big as hills," and "peaceful as the moon." Her gift to them, a yellow flower, is now being reciprocated. Her great-uncle had said that waiting for the whales to come was a waste of time, a foolish endeavor. But Lilly is truly her grandmother's girl, a believer in the power of magic and nature.

In *Moonlight on the River* (Kovacs), two brothers, Will and Ben, sneak out into the night to go on their own private fishing excursion. Navigating their sailboat requires concentration and steady hands, but these two are experienced sailors, very much at ease on the water. In fact, they see the river as an extension of their home and know many of its secrets and moods.

The two boys are also keen observers, and on this, their all-night journey, they spot a great blue heron, a number of circling bluefish, and small glowing water creatures, beautiful and hypnotic.

Later, though, the gentle night breezes become snapping winds. The water rises, then whips and rages, stealing their food and all the clothes they are not wearing. A stranger in another boat points them toward safety, and the two are forced to spend the night in a cove beneath a canvas tarp where they are protected from the rain and chill.

The next morning, as they sail home, the water is calm. Exhilarated and relieved, they return to the safety of their bedroom and the warmth and dryness it provides.

But the journey has been worth everything—worth being cold and worth, if it were to happen, being scolded or punished. After all, they are returning in triumph with a five-pound bluefish souvenir. As children of the river, this was their rite of passage and something they felt compelled to do.

Journeys in the night can be fraught with all kinds of peril. Alemayu, the heroic young dreamer in *Fire on the Mountain* (Kurtz), bets the rich man whom he works for that he can spend the night on a severe, impossible mountain with "only a shemma wrapped around him and a flute in his hand." However, this rich man of ugly moods is certain Alemayu will die or return after just a few hours.

The night is especially harsh, but this bright Ethiopian boy has incredible resolve. He combats the wind's lash and chill by playing his music. Even with hyenas encircling him and the wind penetrating his face and hands, he remains focused on a shepherd's fire on the neighboring mountain. "I kept my eyes on the red glow in the distance, and dreamed of being warm, and that is how I had the strength to survive."

My Freedom Trip (Park) documents a young Korean girl's efforts to escape to South Korea with her guide, Mr. Han, before the start of the Korean War. She must separate from her mother, who will be coming later, and try to reunite with her father at the journey's end, if she can make it safely, across the river at the border.

This is a story about how one child named Soo must deal with upheaval, loss, and overwhelming changes. Feeling torn and divided, with her loving parents now in two different places, she must store all her feelings inside and remain stoic and calm.

As Soo and Mr. Han travel at night up the mountains, they must conceal themselves at all times, hiding in the bushes and rocks when the moon's light is too strong. Even slight shadow movements could give them away.

For Soo, the long silences are hard, and the terrain is rough. Soldiers scour the area, and wild animals moan and cry, piercing the night and unsettling her. How does she deal with moments of danger, and how does she sustain her courage and hope? When Soo and Mr. Han are discovered by a soldier right near the river, will he let her continue or force her to return?

When the soldier whispers, "Go quickly, child," Soo can at last breathe again and release her feelings. She can now "rush into the river, embracing the sun and sky." The night has ended, and her father is waiting.

In the World War II story *The Power of Light* (Singer, I.), 14-year-old David goes scavenging for food in the Warsaw Ghetto, where he could be either captured or killed or hurt by "mortar and falling bricks." When he returns to his beloved Rebecca in the safe harbor of their collapsed cellar, he brings with him both food and treasure—the treasure being a Hanukkah candle and several matches. As David lights and blesses the candle on this, the first night of the Jewish holiday, the glow of the candle reveals his "face streaked with dirt and his eyes filled with tears."

This image touches Rebecca and seems to transform her. It is at this moment that she feels ready to begin their escape, their odyssey to freedom. The light in this story gives her the courage to be decisive, to take action, and to move on. It is a light of hope and renewal, one that links her spiritually to her family and culture.

In contrast to the light of the candle is the ominous Nazi searchlight, invasive and menacing, ruling the night. It is an ugly, monstrous eye arousing sharp pangs of terror in those like David and Rebecca who must constantly remain in hiding.

Creative Excursions

A Bedtime Survey.   Younger children could poll other children about bedtime and then make colorful graphs and charts to illustrate their findings. How many have a dream catcher or a music box? How many eat a bedtime snack? How many sleep with a teddy bear or another stuffed animal? How many sleep alone? How many sleep with siblings?

Night Creatures.   After viewing John and Faith Hubley's *Moonbird,* younger children could create drawings and paintings of other elusive night creatures, perhaps a night elf or a star toad. They could then develop stories or plays about these characters.

My Perfect Bedroom.   Younger or middle-grade children could design and then, in miniature, make their own ideal bedroom by using shoe boxes, carpet scraps, and wallpaper samples. Some might prefer to make peep worlds of famous bedrooms in children's books—the dorm-style bedroom of Madeline (Bemelman), the charming, small-scale bedroom of Stuart Little (White), or the cluttered and crowded bedroom where Charlie Bucket's four grandparents all sleep in one bed (Dahl).

An Exhibit of Moon Masks.   Younger or middle-grade children could listen to various tales in which the moon is an important character or key element and then create paper or papier-mâché masks bringing to life their own interpretations of a moon described in a particular story. The exhibition should feature a range of moons with many different dispositions. Some story possibilities are *The Angry Moon* (Sleator), *Owl Moon* (Yolen), and *The Moon's Revenge* (Aiken).

A Moon Feast.   Younger or middle-grade children could prepare and cook special foods described in *Day of the Dead* (Johnston) and *Moon Festival* (Russell). Both of these books focus on nighttime celebrations that involve songs and dances, stories and prayers, and families and communities reuniting. One group could make Mexican treats such as empanadas, sugar skulls, and mole—an intoxicating blend of chocolate and chili. A second group could prepare the Chinese foods introduced in *Moon Festival*–roast pork and golden moon cakes. A third group could create lanterns, masks, and other decorations.

Late-Night Encounters. Pairs of middle-grade children could improvise, through dramatic play, their imagined encounters with any of the famous or mythical night characters including the BFG (Dahl), The Headless Horseman (Irving), the Tomten (Lindgren), and The Dream Stealer (Maguire).

Researching Bedtime Rituals. Middle-grade children could find information about the bedtime rituals that families observe–from telling stories to saying prayers to wishing on stars. They could interview parents and grandparents to find out the childhood rituals that they remember. They could investigate to see if there are different bedtime rituals in different parts of the world. Some children may want to develop a picture book on this subject or create bedtime rituals of their own.

Lullaby Time. Middle-grade children could collect lullabies from around the world and record the ones sung to them by parents and grandparents. They could then learn to sing these lullabies or play the melodies on a recorder or flute. Some children might want to compose their own night songs, perhaps one about a mischievous moon ray, a teddy bear that keeps belching, or a hammock that transports a child to a magical land.

Stories of the Night. Middle-grade children could collect and share bedtime stories–including camp tales, folk and fairy tales, and Native American myths about the moon and stars and late evening sky. Some children may want to create their own original night tales. These tales could be about the world's first bedtime story, an adamant girl who refuses to go to sleep, a young wizard and his missing moon bucket, or a giant, three-foot bedtime chicken that pops up nightly to disrupt the lives of one family. Some children could design a paper story quilt with each section illustrating a character of the night. These characters might include Hildilid (Ryan), The Sandman (Shepperson), The Tomten (Lindgren), Grandfather Twilight (Berger), and Mickey from *In the Night Kitchen* (Sendak).

A Sleeping Scroll. Middle-grade children could research information about sleeping. They could then devise a scroll that would contain the information found combined with their own original drawings. Among questions they might want to pursue are: What makes a child drowsy at night? What happens to someone's brain, heart, and muscles when they are sleeping? Why do babies sleep so much and older people sleep so little? Why do some children snore, grind their teeth, or walk in their sleep? What causes children to dream? Do animals dream? Which animals sleep upside down or standing on one leg?

A Circle of Dreamers. Sitting in a ceremonial circle, middle-grade children could take turns sharing their dreams, recalling important images and events.

They would need to describe the people in their dream, where the dream took place, and the feelings they experienced.

A Dream Gallery.   Middle-grade children could develop a special gallery that would feature drawings and paintings of their most powerful dreams. Each of their dreamscapes might have a title and a short, poetic description. Also on display could be the children's own interpretive illustrations of such dream books as *In the Night Kitchen* (Sendak), *Ben's Dream* (Van Allsburg), *Tree of Dreams* (Yep), *The Dream Stealer* (Maguire), *Coyote Dreams* (Nunes), *The Night Flight* (Ryder), *Where Did All the Dragons Go?* (Robinson), and *Free Fall* (Wiesner).

Illuminated Story Boxes.   Middle-grade or older children, working in small groups, could create dioramas showing a three-dimensional night scene from a favorite story. After making the model sets and figures, their next challenge would be to illuminate their boxes, perhaps using tiny electric lights or a flashlight. They might, for example, depict the scene where Peter Pan and his new friends go soaring over the dazzle of lights of a late-night London.

The Mysterious Light.   What if one were to see signals flashing from a lighthouse at night even though no one was inside? What if one were to see an orange oblong light hovering over a bridge and then suddenly moving away at an incredible speed? Middle-grade and older children could write original tales about a strange, beckoning, and elusive light. Where does the light come from? What are its color and intensity? Does it have a special power? Does it lead them to an unusual place or a fantastic world? Can others see the light as well? Children could share their stories in a candlelight ceremony.

A Film Discussion.   Older children, after viewing the 1955 classic *The Night of the Hunter*, could examine the elements that contribute to its stark mood and unrelenting terror. In this film, a brother and sister are living in the time of the Great Depression. They journey into the night to flee from their stepfather, a fraudulent preacher who has murdered their mother and now pursues them for their money. The night in this film has a poetic beauty, but it brings little peace to these two children. Whenever they begin to feel a measure of safety or try to sleep, they hear his hymns as he rides after them on horseback. He is their nightmare, steely and hypnotic, taking his time and moving in closer and closer.

Resources

Books

Ackerman, Karen. *By the Dawn's Early Light.* Atheneum, 1994.
Aiken, Joan. *The Moon's Revenge.* Knopf, 1987.
Arnold, Todd. *No Jumping on the Bed.* Dial, 1987.
Arrigg, Fred. *The Baseball Star.* Troll, 1995.

Artis, Vicki. *Pajama Walking.* Houghton, 1981.

Bauer, Marion. *When I Go Camping with Grandma.* Bridgewater, 1995.

Bemelman, Ludwig. *Madeline.* Puffin, 1977.

Berger, Barbara. *Grandfather Twilight.* Philomel, 1984.

Brinckloe, Julie. *Fireflies!* Aladdin, 1985.

Brown, Margaret Wise. *Goodnight, Moon.* Harper, 1974.

Carlstrom, Nancy. *Northern Lullaby.* Philomel, 1992.

Dahl, Roald. *The BFG.* Farrar, 1982.

Engvick, William. *Lullabies and Night Songs.* Harper, 1965.

Goron, Maria. *Day and Night.* Thomson, 1995.

Greenfield, Eloise. *Night on Neighborhood Street.* Dial, 1991.

Heckman, Philip. *The Moon Is Following Me.* Atheneum, 1990.

Himmelman, John. *Lights Out!* Bridgewater, 1995.

Ho, Minfong. *Hush! A Thai Lullaby.* Orchard, 1996.

Hodges, Margaret. *The Fire Bringer.* Little, 1972.

Hurd, Edith T. *I Dance in My Red Pajamas.* Harper, 1982.

Irving, Washington. *The Legend of Sleepy Hollow.* Wildside, 2004.

Isom, Joan. *The First Starry Night.* Whispering, 1997.

Johnson, Angela. *Tell Me a Story, Mama.* Orchard, 1989.

Johnston, Tony. *The Day of the Dead.* Harcourt, 1997.

Karlin, Bernie. *Night Ride.* Atheneum, 1984.

Kaye, Marilyn. *The Real Tooth Fairy.* Harcourt, 1990.

Kovacs, Deborah. *Moonlight on the River.* Viking, 1993.

Kurtz, Jane. *Fire on the Mountain.* Simon, 1994.

Lasky, Kathryn. *The Night Journey.* Warne, 1982.

Lindgren, Astrid. *I Don't Want to Go to Bed.* R & S, 1988.

Lindgren, Astrid. *The Tomten.* Coward, 1961.

Loh, Morag. *Tucking Mommy In.* Orchard, 1981.

Maguire, Gregory. *The Dream Stealer.* Harper, 1983.

Martin, Jr., Bill. *Knots on a Counting Rope.* Holt, 1987.

Mayer, Mercer. *There's a Nightmare in My Closet.* Dial, 1986.

Mayo, Gretchen. *Star Tales.* Walker, 1987.

McCauley, Jan. *Ways Animals Sleep.* National Geographic, 1983.

Nunes, Susan. *Coyote Dreams.* Atheneum, 1988.

Ormerod, Jan. *Moonlight.* Lothrop, 1982.

Park, Barbara. *My Freedom Trip.* Boyds, 1998.

Robinson, Fay. *Where Did All the Dragons Go?* Bridgewater, 1996.

Roop, Peter. *Keep the Lights Burning, Abbie.* Carolrhoda, 1985.

Russell, Ching Young. *Moon Fesival.* Boyds, 1997.

Ryan, Cheli D. *Hildilid's Night.* Macmillan, 1971.

Ryder, Joanne. *The Night Flight.* Four Winds, 1985.

Sendak, Maurice. *In the Night Kitchen.* Harper, 1970.

Shannon, David. *No, David!* Blue Sky, 1998.

Sheldon, Dyan. *The Whale's Song.* Puffin, 1990.

Shepperson, Rob. *The Sandman.* Farrar, 1990.

Showers, Paul. *Sleep Is for Everyone.* Harper, 1972.

Singer, Isaac. *The Power of Light: Eight Stories for Hannukah.* Farrar, 1980.

Singer, Marilyn. *Nine O'Clock Lullaby*. Harper, 1991.

Sleator, William. *The Angry Moon*. Little, 1970.

Snyder, Zilpha. *Blair's Nightmare*. Atheneum, 1984.

Van Allsburg, Chris. *Ben's Dream*. Houghton, 1988.

Van Allsburg, Chris. *The Mysteries of Harris Burdick*. Houghton, 1984.

Waber, Bernard. *A Firefly Named Torchy*. Houghton, 1970.

Waber, Bernard. *Ira Sleeps Over*. Houghton, 1972.

White, E. B. *Stuart Little*. Harper, 1973.

Wiesner, David. *Free Fall*. Scholastic, 1988.

Willard, Nancy. *Nightgown for the Sullen Moon*. Harcourt, 1983.

Yep, Laurence. *Tree of Dreams*. Bridgewater, 1995.

Yolen, Jane. *Owl Moon*. Philomel, 1987.

Yolen, Jane. *Sleep Rhymes around the World*. Wordsong, 1994.

Zolotow, Charlotte. *The Sleepy Book*. Harper, 1988.

Films, Videos, and DVDs

All Summer in a Day. Corporation, 1982. 16 minutes.

Close Encounters of the Third Kind, directed by Steven Spielberg. Columbia, 1983. 134 minutes.

The Fur Coat Club. Learning Corporation, 1973. 19 minutes.

Moonbird. McGraw-Hill, 1959. 10 minutes.

The Night of the Hunter, directed by Charles Laughton. United Artists, 1955. 93 minutes.

A Few Reflections

Besides all the intrinsic rewards that may come from engaging children in thematic journeys, there are sometimes those paper treasures, frayed yet tangible, that show you how important these programs can be. Such items received from children may include a poem, a drawing, a thoughtful piece of writing.

Often these paper treasures reveal what children take away from their experiences with you or even how they apply these experiences years later. As measures of what you are trying to achieve, they can help you to see what children have absorbed and valued.

A 10-year-old boy writing about his experience transforming the Corlears library media center into a makeshift circus reveals not only his pride and self-esteem but also his sense of being challenged.

When I started my mime act, I felt nervous and scared. I didn't know how to start. But when I made my first movements, I felt sensational. I really wanted to participate. So I said to myself, "Give it your best, Derrick." It came out wonderful. I wanted to give them an encore. I wanted the people that watched to leave satisfied. I wanted them to be impressed.

Derrick Vandyck

Ten-year-olds involved in creating the Corlears Colonial Workshop wrote about their experiences as master apprentices teaching younger children some of the specific skills involved in weaving, tile making, candle making, and pottery.

Through this project, many considered for the first time what it would be like to prepare and develop a lesson and to try to spark the curiosity of their charges. They were continually assessing and problem solving. "What is the best way to convey my idea, to teach my lesson, to sustain the younger kids' interest?" As teachers, they seemed to have the flexibility to shift gears whenever necessary, and as collaborators, they were able to divide the labor and work out their partnerships.

Overall, their tone was gentle, earnest, and lighthearted. There was always the sharing of excitement, and most kids acknowledged that teaching could be a very intense experience. It was clear how much they valued humor, often using it as a tool to make a point, defuse a situation, or help a younger child feel more comfortable.

In their writings, they described their joys and difficulties and their sense of anticipation.

....

Before the kids came, I was a little nervous because I didn't know if it would all run smoothly or not. After the first class came, I knew what to do with the next class.

Jessica Bradley

I wondered if the kids would be hyper or squirrelly. I wondered if they would break any tiles. I hoped all the teachers would cope. Mostly we did.

Abigail Dugan

I was patient. I had to talk very slowly. I had to make them pay attention.

Maximillian Saint-Preux

I was pretty patient. I was as friendly as I could be without being sickeningly sweet.

Hannah Silverman

In candle-making, one girl named Galen said she was scared to make a candle. I had to talk to her a lot for her to make one candle. I felt proud to help her. Then she felt more confident.

Aliza Holmes

....

Some paper treasures can touch you quite deeply. They may come years later, unexpectedly, from former students, letting you know that it all mattered and that they understood your purpose or vision. I received the following poem from a 17-year-old heading off for his first year of college. What a magical and inventive kid he was, and I had often wondered what ways he would move in the world and what extraordinary things he would surely create.

....

There's an eavesdropping star
and I wonder Gary
where you are.
I imagine you
among the
forests or the mountains
that we drew
when you instructed us
to create worlds.
I wonder if you know how
many lives you touched
with your trembling hands.
no one understands
when I tell them that my
best friend
was a librarian.
your library on the
third floor
was never quiet,
always filled with laughter and turning minds,
always filled with you.
it was your universe
where all of our worlds
flew around.
where are you now
Gary?
where
are
you
now?
thanks.
thanks for exposing
me to myself.
thanks for all the
laughter that made
school enjoyable.
thanks for being a friend.

Halsey Chait

....

INDEX ·· ●

About the Author

GARY ZINGHER has engaged children in thematic journeys in a number of settings. He has been the library media specialist at Corlears School, Manhattan Country School, and Bank Street College Children's School; the imagination consultant at the Children's Workshop School; a play therapist at St. Luke's Hospital; and the creative arts director at Camp Vacamas in West Milford, New Jersey. He codeveloped and cotaught the New Perspectives course "Creative Library Programs for Children" at the Bank Street College of Education and has led imagination workshops at Columbia Teacher's College, Pacific Oaks College, St. John's University, and the University of Missouri at Kansas City. He is the author of *At the Pirate Academy: Adventures with Language in the Library Media Center,* published by the American Library Association (1990), and his column "Thematic Journeys" appears in *School Library Media Activities Monthly.* He also writes for *Crinkles* and *Novelist.*